THE AUTOBIOGRAPHY
OF AN ATTITUDE

THE BOOKS OF GEORGE JEAN NATHAN

The Theatre

THE CRITIC AND THE DRAMA*
THE POPULAR THEATRE
MATERIA CRITICA
MR. GEORGE JEAN NATHAN PRESENTS
COMEDIANS ALL
ANOTHER BOOK ON THE THEATRE
THE THEATRE, THE DRAMA, THE GIRLS

Satire

A BOOK WITHOUT A TITLE
BOTTOMS UP

Plays

HELIOGABALUS (in collaboration with H. L. Mencken)**

Philosophy

THE AUTOBIOGRAPHY OF AN ATTITUDE
THE AMERICAN CREDO: A CONTRIBUTION TOWARD THE INTERPRE-
TATION OF THE NATIONAL MIND (in collaboration with H. L.
Mencken)

Art and Life

THE WORLD IN FALSEFACE*

Travel and Reminiscence

EUROPE AFTER 8:15 * (in collaboration with H. L. Mencken)

In Collaborative Compilations

CIVILIZATION IN THE UNITED STATES, by Thirty Americans
ESSAYS BY PRESENT-DAY WRITERS, by Raymond Woodbury Pence
READINGS FROM "THE AMERICAN MERCURY," by Grant. C. Knight

* Also published in Great Britain
** Also published in Germany

THE AUTOBIOGRAPHY
· OF AN ATTITUDE ·

GEORGE   JEAN   NATHAN

New York   ALFRED · A · KNOPF   Mcmxxv

"There are more things in heaven and earth, Horatio, than are dreamt of in your philosophy."—*Hamlet*.

CONTENTS

CONTENTS

THE AUTOBIOGRAPHY
OF AN ATTITUDE

I. PERSONAL ATTITUDE

§ 1

Outline of the History of a Man's Philosophical Knowledge from Early Youth to Old Age.—
1. I am wrong. 2. I am right. 3. I am wrong.

§ 2

A man's philosophy, his attitude toward the world, is very seldom found to be the result of carefully reasoned reflection, meditation and deduction. It is, to the contrary, generally the largely fortuitous end-product and sum-product of a hundred and one extra-subjective occurrences, adventures and phenomena that have figured in his life. A man's immediate philosophy thus has infinitely less relation to cold intellect and shrewd penetration than to how much money he happens to have in the bank, how thin his hair is on top, how biologically spry he is when he wakes up in the morning, how much he has swindled his partner out of, or vice versa, how his last girl has treated him, and how much genuine Piesporter he has left in his cellar.

There may be, true enough, men whose philosophical attitudes toward the world are removed from such things, whose doctrines and views are direct descendants of the cerebral centres, uncontaminated by the passing humors and megrims of life or by personal triumphs and despairs. But they are surely few and far between. Even the worldly philosophy of the greatest of our rationalists has doubtless been conditioned much more than we suspect by extra-metaphysical eventualities. To penetrate to the genesis of the divers philosophies of these presumably august and secluded fellows, we should, as I have hinted in the past, first ferret out their immediate state and condition of life, mind, health, heart and finance at the time when they conceived and recorded their contributions to the wisdom of the world. What, in other words, were the provoking causes, the psychological bricks, the personal influences that figured in the rearing of their attitudes toward the cosmos? For example, what was Nietzsche's blood pressure and how hard was his tailor pressing him when he wrote "Human All-Too-Human"? What had Schopenhauer's pet chamber-maid, Gusti, just done to him when he sat down to his essay on women? What—I have often speculated—was the

4

exact relationship of John Stuart Mill and his wife at the time he composed his celebrated paper on the subjection of the female of the species? What did Spencer eat and drink, and did his physician compel him to wear flannel underwear, and, if so, did it tickle? What—as I have asked a thousand times, with no satisfactory answer forthcoming—did Darwin's mother-in-law look like at the time he first thought of his theory of evolution?

The generality of men, indeed, great and small, are not so much the fathers of their worldly philosophy as the children. Their attitude toward life and their fellow men is not born in them, it is thrust upon them. If a man hasn't a cent in the world one day and suddenly comes into twenty thousand dollars the next, he is not the same man, and his philosophy is not the same philosophy. If a man's wife runs away with the family osteopath at five-fifteen one afternoon, the man's five-ten philosophical attitude toward the globe we inhabit is as dead as a wet tennis ball. Man in the mass derives his view of the world from what the world does to him. His mind is not a free agent, but one in thrall to a thousand external happenings. Cleopatra's nose changed the history of the world no more than a defective sinus frequently changes the history of men's attitudes toward the world. If Walt Whit-

5

man had owned an extra pair of pants he would
have been a royalist.

§ 3

What is my own philosophy of life? It is, in
simple, merely this: to forget the miseries of the
past and remember only its charm, to live the present to the limit of its utmost possibilities, and to
view the future as one who has traveled romantically in a colorful far country views the skyline of
his nearing homeland—with a sense of great content and slightly sad resignation.

§ 4

The older I grow, the more I am persuaded that
hedonism is the only sound and practical doctrine
of faith for the intelligent man. I doubt, indeed,
if there ever has lived an intelligent man whose end
in life was not the achievement of a large and selfish pleasure. This latter is often shrewdly
swathed in the deceptive silks of altruism or what
not, but brush the silks aside and the truth of self-
gratification is visible in all its nudity. Mohammed's altruism was as completely hedonistic as
Charlemagne's frank hedonism. The greater the
idealist, the greater the hedonist behind the whiskers.

Altruism, it seems to me, is the highest flowering of selfishness. In the heart of the greatest altruist one will always find the largest mirror. The history of altruism is a long series of self-engraved, adulatory epitaphs.

§ 5

I find, upon honest reflection, that I am uplifted not by my virtues, but by my vices. They cheer me, make me happy and contented, make life seem worth while when my day's work is done, send the blood of tonic joy shooting through my veins, banish blueness and self-doubt and worry and despond.

§ 6

I am not what is generally known as the popular type of man. That is, I am not the sort of man who is liked by the majority of persons with whom he comes into contact. I have a number of very good friends, among both men and women; but, aside from these, the general run of people whose paths cross my own are of as little personal interest to me as I am, assuredly, to them. I am not interesting to these persons because I prefer their disinterest, and am at no pains to conceal it. I know and always feel that it would be the simplest thing in the world to provoke their interest, at least to a degree—a technic grantedly not occult—but I am not able to persuade myself that their interest in me, the one way or the other, is worth concerning myself with. If I like a person, he or she knows it; I show my interest at once. If I don't care for a person, he or she knows it just as quickly; the lack of interest on my part is at once obvious.

All this makes for unpopularity. To be popular, one must show interest in persons and things that do not interest one and simultaneously conceal the interest that one has in persons and things that do interest one. One must always side with the prejudices and emotions of the person one happens to be with, however idiotic. One must laugh when one doesn't feel like it; be quiet when one would be gay. One must tell old women one loves them, and young women one doesn't. One must be humorous but never witty, interested but never enthusiastic, complacently bored but never tired. When one is with one's intellectual inferiors, one must agreeably reduce one's self not to the level of these others, but below that level, that they may have the comfortable feeling of being at complete conversational ease. One must be privy to the trick of flattering another person's vanity by contradicting what he says and then allowing him to convince one that he is right. One must pretend to take lightly what one feels about most profoundly.

8

One may be original in manner, but never in thought.

I am able to negotiate all these things, but I decline to do so. Among the many millions of persons in this fair land, there are not more than a dozen at the very outside, who, known to me personally, interest me personally in the slightest. The rest, so far as I am concerned, can go chase themselves.

§ 7

Nothing is so challengeful as a defence of one's self. Nothing is so disarming as the custom of admitting everything.

§ 8

Every time I hear a man pound a table with his fist and loudly endorse common sense I permit myself a pianissimo hiccup. What, I ask myself, is this much lauded common sense? Is it the absolute thing it is believed to be? Has the phrase, indeed, any common sense in it? The answer is no. Common sense is what any man, however doltish, believes it to be. What one man regards as common sense, further, another man, equally intelligent, does not regard as common sense. The common sense of one generation is often found to be

9

the nonsense of the next generation. It is as variable as the wind. Common sense, in short, is frequently nothing more than a name for a man's foolish conviction that what he thinks is right. Is there such a thing as absolute truth? Is there such a thing as absolute common sense? No prize is offered for the correct answer.

Common sense, in so far as it exists at all, is for the bourgeoisie. Nonsense is the privilege of the aristocracy. The worries of the world are for the common people. Meanwhile the elect may amuse and divert itself with tzigane philosophies and Puckish metaphysics. Only the cultivated, the well-to-do and the secure are safe and free to indulge themselves in holidays from acumen.

§ 9

I am a relatively happy and contented man. Therefore, I often act in ways and do things that others less fortunate than I consider unseemly and foolish.

Of all human emotions, this one of contentment, is, however, the most puzzling. The contentment of other people I can often understand no better than I can understand my own. Why should contentment, the glorious harbor of the wearied mind and heart and soul of mortal man which should be reached only with the very greatest difficulty—why should this contentment so often be achieved, as it is achieved, through means of such childish simplicity and with such apparent ease? Is it because of all emotions contentment is the most transitory, that it is comparatively only of the moment, for the moment and by the moment? Consider. There is no person who, for all his travail, does not achieve contentment many, many times during his life. It is, in point of fact, the one emotion, the one sensation, that he experiences the least trouble with. He may never achieve a woman's love, or a worth-while man's bracing hate, or a sweet grief, or supreme happiness, or the sense of power—any of the emotional satisfactions or paradoxically satisfactory dissatisfactions of life on earth, but contentment is none the less periodically his. In this lies the secret of man's smiling acceptance and endurance of his fate, whatever its nature. In his many little contentments rests life's apologia to him. A letter of pleasant promise that is destined never to be fulfilled, a decent meal with a cigar that burns evenly, the passing smile of a pretty girl, a successful petty swindle, the failure of an anticipated embarrassment to materialize, the mellifluous effect of a couple of whiskeys and soda, a pair of surprisingly comfortable new shoes, the first well day after an illness—in such things, most

11

of them of an obvious triviality, lies the seed of man's temporary complacency and happiness. For the moment he is reconciled with life; for the moment the rags of his ache and worldly disappointment are concealed beneath the ermine of a refulgent mirage.

As for happiness, on the other hand, the trouble with it is that it generally comes to one too early in life. I speak, of course, of the sensation of happiness, not happiness in its permanence which, equally of course, is a bird so rare as to be almost non-existent. In youth there are many more moments of happiness than there are in later years; youth is made happy by things that age is not; it is more easily tickled and satisfied by those phenomena of life that produce what passes for happiness. To be made happy, age demands phenomena increasingly novel and vastly more complex. As sensations decrease in power with repetition, happiness thus becomes a weaker and weaker emotion as life goes on. It suffers a discounting; the warmth that it leaves as its residuum becomes less and less warm. The happiness of a little boy over a Christmas stocking filled with peppermint candy, tangerine oranges and pretty tissue paper cornucopias, were it susceptible of psychological laboratory analysis, would be found to be of six times the voltage of the happiness of the same little boy, now arrived at the age of fifty, who had just achieved his millionth dollar.

§ 10

The world is not run equitably. I have got a lot more from it than I know I actually deserve.

§ 11

It is utterly impossible for a poverty-stricken man to understand my point of view. Thus, I never pay the slightest attention to criticisms of my writings from men condemned to miserable lives.

This is an unpleasant and doubtless objectionable statement. But it happens to be the way I feel in the matter.

§ 12

Time, commonly regarded as a tragedian, is actually a comedian. The tragedies that time brings with its passing are puny in number and degree compared with the comedies and burlesque shows. No man, looking back across the years of his life, can fail to discern the unsuspected humors that time has found there and brought to light. Time is the greatest of comic dramatists. The moment the curtain falls on one of its tragedies, it begins to satirize it.

13

§ 13

Cynicism is less often the fruit of failure than of success. The man who has failed has still in his heart all of his aspirations and dreams, that yet seem to him brave and worth-while and glamorous. The cynicism of such a man is essentially dishonest. But the man who has succeeded has no aspirations and no dreams left to him. He has realized them and, having realized them, has found them out for the relatively petty things they are. His cynicism is, accordingly, at once the more sound and the more sincere.

§ 14

The prejudice of the general run of people is not so much against the man who thinks differently from itself as against the one who feels differently. General opinion, while it may not view with favor the man who entertains philosophies and ideas oppugnant to its own, nevertheless treats him with more or less poise and charity. But the man whose emotions differ radically from its own, whose feelings are not so greatly standardized as its own feelings, the public make short shrift of. It brushes him aside in distrust and dislike, and bestows upon him a parting hinter-boot. The man with ideas other than its ideas the public puts down merely as something of a misled fool. But the man with emotions other than its own emotions it puts down as a dangerous and suspicious fellow, and one to be treated as a typhus bacillus.

P. S. The world respects the man who smashes its philosophical illusions, but it despises the man who smashes its emotional ones.

§ 15

Speaking of illusions, it yet remains that as many of the great battles of the world are won by a blind following of illusion as by a realistic facing of facts. The illusion of Joan of Arc's sainthood drew the French to victory over the English in the Fifteenth Century as the illusion of democracy drew the American colonists to triumph over the English in the Eighteenth. The first Crusaders, sweeping in a trail of white glory toward the East, were carried along on the invincible shoulders of divine illusion and it was only when the purple illusion of Cleopatra's love deserted him that Mark Antony met defeat at arms; under the warm spell of that illusion he defeated both Brutus and Cassius at Philippi. It was the illusion that Thomas Jonathan Jackson was like a stone wall that led his soldiers in gray to stand like rocks and bounce back to threefold defeat the men in blue who, without a similar illusion to support them, followed McDowell at Bull Run and Banks at Winchester and Cedar Mountain.

§ 16

There is no need for philosophy in youth. Philosophy is age's apology for itself, a soft mattress for its fading and again uncapturable resources.

§ 17

The world is divided into householders and gypsies. I have no other use for the former than to use them to the advantage of my own pleasure or material profit. They are often estimable and to be respected—and in some ways I envy them— but there is to me in them inevitably a touch of narrowness and romantic sordidness that I do not like. Therefore, I crack the whip of my humor upon them, as a circus ringmaster cracks his upon a troupe of amusing, almost human, and quite pitiable monkeys.

§ 18

To be doubtful of many things, but never of one's self—such is the doctrine of success.

§ 19

Great philosophers are often as guilty of saying foolish things as the rest of us. I cull, in illustration, the following samples from the dicta of the estimable Friedrich Wilhelm Nietzsche:

1. "A man of genius is unbearable unless he possess at least two things besides: gratitude and purity".

2. "The thought of suicide is a great consolation: by means of it one gets successfully through many a bad night".

3. "In praise there is more obtrusiveness than in blame".

4. "One does not believe in the follies of clever men: what a forfeiture of the rights of man!"

5. "The only decisive argument that has always deterred men from drinking a poison is not that it is deadly, but that it has an unpleasant taste".

6. "We simulate pity when we wish to show ourselves superior to the feeling of animosity, but generally in vain".

I have quoted but half a dozen titbits. There are many more.

§ 20

I am not a pacifist; I believe in wars. I am not a matador; but I believe in bull-fights.

§ 21

Those things at which a man jests have sometimes the curious trick of becoming his subsequent stoutest faiths.

§ 22

We all in due time are made to pay the penalty of our virtues.

§ 23

The observation that when a given truth survives it is no sign that anyone has cherished it over a given duration of time, but simply a sign that believers in it have succeeded one another in an unbroken succession—this observation seems to me to be one of the few truths of which a careful man may say without qualification that it is substantially true. What I believed in 1910 I no longer believe, but some one else *does* believe it—some pathetic ass. Thus every truth with any merit in it whatsoever is kept alive. As one crowd of believers goes out, another comes in.

§ 24

The truth is whatever falsehood makes the most profound impression on us. The pursuit of truth

consists simply in running away from a swiftly
pursuing pack of lies, with the latter gaining
ground constantly.

§ 25

Ambition is a commendable thing, but too much
pious nonsense has been preached about it. The
ambitions of all of us should properly be bounded
by a critical appreciation of our own limitations.
I, for example, should like nothing better than to
be able to afford the ambition to write criticism
as profound and as fine as John Dryden's, but I
have enough critical instinct to know that such an
achievement is beyond my capabilities.

§ 26

As I grow older, I notice that the word "perhaps"
begins to appear more and more often in my critical writings. I am perhaps not so sure of the
truth of what I believe as I once was.

§ 27

When a man tells me that he has seen this or
that old friend of mine and that he or she is very

happy, I pause to reflect upon my informant's concept of happiness as opposed to my own.

§ 28

I do not care to hear what other persons think of me.   They may be right.

II. ATTITUDE TOWARD THEOLOGY

§ 1

Jesus Christ was born in 6 B.C. The Right Rev. William T. Manning, S.T.D., D.D., LL.D., was born in 1866 A.D. How time flies!

§ 2

To be thoroughly religious, one must be sorely disappointed. One's faith in God increases as one's faith in the world decreases. The happier the man or woman, the farther he or she is from God.

§ 3

Picture time turned hind end foremost, and the world with it. Picture then a Buddha born not at the foot of the Nepalese Himalayas but at No.4 Wu Wu Street, Pekin, a Mohammed born not at Mecca but in a boarding-house near the railroad station in Constantinople, a Christ born not in Bethlehem, Palestine, but in Bethlehem, Pennsylvania, a Moses getting his message on one of the

Catskill mountains. . . . How many churches, thus unsupported by the mystery and romance of distance, would not promptly be converted into "Dreamland" dance halls and moving picture parlors?

§ 4

The agnostic can find much to support his philosophy in the nearest drugstore. Countless beauty preparations to bring beauty where beauty is lacking, illimitable correctives against unseemly defects in the human body, inside and out, a thousand and one tonics to build up the weak and fragile and imperfect human machine, innumerable drugs and chemicals to keep the body temporarily safe from the threatenings of Fate—shelf upon shelf of criticisms and denials of an All-Merciful and an Almighty. Every druggist is *ipso facto* the propagandist of an infidel doctrine.

§ 5

Mammon, they tell us, is a poor God. But is It? Isn't It the kindest, the least selfish, the most greatly contributive to happiness, the most comfortably visible, the most beneficent and most practical of all the gods? Does It not give one power, and remove self-doubt, and cheer the spirit, and give one a pervading faith? Does It not make of life a spectacle of color, and banish fear, and instil in one a great tolerance and generosity? Does It not make one gentler toward one's enemies, and staunch in the face of disappointments, and solicitous of the poor and humble, and bring one to look on the world with more understanding and sympathetic eyes? Does It not make one's family happy and insure ease and happiness to one's children? Does It not baffle ill health and misery, in so far as anything can baffle them? Does It not, finally, bring even the skeptic to believe in the goodness and wisdom of another and even greater God?

§ 6

The Tenth Commandment: the theological Monroe Doctrine.

§ 7

Although I believe in ghosts no more than I believe in democracy or cures for neuralgia in the eyeball, some of the arguments against them currently vouchsafed by skeptics do not entirely persuade me. One of the favorite of these arguments, the chief in fact, is, for example, that if spirits really exist and can get into communication with

23

the living, why don't they tell something worth while instead of confining themselves to such obvious pieces of news as: Uncle Milt is very happy in Heaven and Benvenuto Cellini is not among those present. Let us say that the ghost speaking is that of Mr. Sigmund Dusenblatt, late of Dusenblatt, Muschel and Glaubman, Inc., Ladies' Cloaks and Suits, and late husband to Mrs. Amanda Dusenblatt, *née* Wiesendinger. The erstwhile M. Dusenblatt during his lifetime was assuredly no raconteur, no walking edition of the *Atlantic Monthly* and *Yellow Book*, no fellow of infinite jest, information and *ésprit*. His conversations with the no less estimable Madame Dusenblatt while he was on earth and a patriotic and active citizen of the Republic were certainly nothing to provoke envy in the breast of a Benjamin Disraeli or an Edmund Gosse. They were confined, doubtless, to the perfectly obvious observations of perfectly obvious gentlemen like himself. Why then, under these circumstances, should it be demanded of the M. Dusenblatt that, dead, he suddenly become gifted with infinite wisdoms, perspicuities and philosophies which were utterly foreign to him while his soul still reposed in his corporeal body? When alive, the M. Dusenblatt undoubtedly sought to convey an emphatic

point to his spouse, to his partners, the talented
MM. Muschel and Glaubman, and to his head
buyer, the statuesque and capable Miss Sheila
O'Toole, by pounding on a table. When dead,
why should not the same M. Dusenblatt pursue the
course that he pursued while alive and seek anal-
ogously to convey his convictions by a necessarily
and inevitably somewhat less obstreperous tapping
on a table?

Or take a ghost of *mise en scène* different from
that of Mr. Dusenblatt. Say the shade of Mr.
Cosmo C. Perkins, the eminent lawyer. Throughout his life, Mr. Perkins confined himself to subtle
evasions, to thumping balderdash and to magnificent prevarications. Why then, now that he is
dead, should his ghost suddenly turn turtle on him
and seek not to evade? Why shouldn't his ghost
go on lying and emitting profound nonsense just
as Cosmo himself did while he was still in a state
of eating mundane Schweitzer cheese sandwiches
and drinking mundane bootleg liquor? If the
ghost of Mr. Perkins, appearing in the darkened
back parlor of Mme. Flora's flat in West 106th
Street, whispers to his trembling widow that he
still loves her, why shouldn't his widow accept it
as an unmistakably accurate proof of after-life,
since surely Mr. Perkins told her the selfsame

thing countless times during his life just after he had returned from important business conferences in Atlantic City with a Follies girl?

Go a step farther. Indeed, go a thousand steps farther. Take the ghost of Napoleon Bonaparte. It is argued by the skeptics that if there really is such a thing as the ghost of Napoleon Bonaparte, that ghost should reasonably be expected to convey more piquant and important information to an expectant world than confining itself merely to the stereotyped spook intelligence that Little Bright Eyes can hear what it is trying to say, that there must be sympathy in the back parlor if it is to get its message across, and that this flabbergastingly important message (subsequently conveyed in the voice of a basso with the No. 3 "Blossom Time" company) is as follows: "It is true that I lost the Battle of Waterloo". Now, what intelligent, logically minded person would reasonably expect the late Napoleon Bonaparte to do anything else? To expect his ghost, after all these years, to turn up in the rear of a two-room, bath and kitchenette apartment in Harlem and confide the inside secrets of his military campaigns to half a dozen former privates in the A.E.F. and their wives is surely to imagine a Napoleon Bonaparte without a sense of humor and deprived of all dignity by the majesty of death. Were he still alive and present in the

26

same company is it conceivable that he would do otherwise than politely confine himself to the same trivialities that the skeptics object to in the case of his ghost? It is not.

The mistake that these skeptics make, it seems to me, lies in assuming that death should completely alter the intrinsic nature of a man, that is, should occultly convert his spirit self into a completely different entity. If I, for instance, should die tomorrow from an overdose of wood alcohol and should turn up as an articulate vapor next Wednesday night in the dining-room of Madame Celeste's flat down in Greenwich Village, what sound reason should there be for expecting me to betray the fact that I had gone to Hell, that there were enough pretty girls down there to give me a very jolly time, and that if I had to live my life over again I should doubtless be just as great a jackass as I had been? Surely the residuum of spurious dignity, of hypocrisy and of talent for euphemism that I had carried with me beyond the grave would restrain me from any such honest and embarrassing admissions. I should certainly slyly content myself and support my late self-esteem with much of the hocus-pocus affected by me during my life-time. I should distract and hornswoggle the assembled intelligentsia with all the familiar and reliable bosh about Wa-Wa, the

27

Indian chief, and the spirit of Julius Cæsar, and should enjoy myself further by tipping the table, striking a tambourine, ringing a bell, and—this most certainly—pinching the leg of the medium. This, after all, is more or less the sort of thing that amused me in life, this is the kind of thing, in the form of literary composition, with which during my life I tormented the yokelry, so why shouldn't I continue to have the same good time now that I was a ghost?   Damned if I know.

§ 8

A wife, a child, a home—these three things, it has been said, round out the completeness and perfection of man.   And to think that the Lord God Almighty Himself has only one of them!

§ 9

Far from getting weaker, it seems to me that the Christian church, if not the Christian religion, is yearly getting stronger and stronger.   It is gaining this strength numerically not because of the doctrines it preaches, not because of the irresistible persuasiveness of its tenets of faith, and not because pagans are becoming honestly converted to it, but, very simply, because it has become increasingly, as year chases year, the fashion and the mode. The Christian church is thus succeeding on a large scale precisely as the Berlitz School's French course is succeeding on a smaller scale. Christianity has, in a manner of speaking, ceased in a measure to be a religion and has become a style. Just as the American, German and French male mammal has long aped the Englishman in the matter of dress and social deportment, so today are an increasing number of infidels, led chiefly by the Jews, aping the Christian in a hundred and one ways. And, since this aping is most convincingly to be negotiated from the inside looking out rather than from the outside looking in, it is the Christian church that has been the benefactor. Things have got to such a pass, indeed, that when a Christian clergyman today speaks from his pulpit the name of Jesus Christ, half the congregation thinks that he is swearing.

§ 10

The fact that certain of the miracles chronicled in the Bible can be explained away by a realistic application of logic is little against them as miracles. It has not been difficult for scientists to analyze the chemistry of flowers, yet for all that no scientist has ever been able to make even a simple white clover. It is the easiest thing in the world

29

for even a corner druggist to tell precisely the composition of Pilsner beer, yet no one this side of the Paradise of Bohemia has ever been able to duplicate that greatest of modern miracles.

§ 11

Although it may prove nothing, there has never been an atheist who didn't secretly like his girl to believe in God.

§ 12

I saw an ambulance rushing a dying man to the hospital held up at Madison Avenue and Forty-Second Street the other night in order to let an eminent Christian Scientist cross the street.

§ 13

In even the least intelligible and harshest religion there is a touch, however small, of beauty. Faith, be it soever ill-founded and vain and ridiculous, has always its measure of beauty. There is something beautiful in even a dog's faith in a Methodist master or a skunk's faith in himself when confronted by a professional moralist.

ATTITUDE TOWARD THEOLOGY

§ 14

I heard four animals carrying on a conversation in English about a friend of theirs, a lamb with seven eyes. I saw a large muscular angel with a book under his arm making several loud remarks. I saw some mountains and islands move themselves about like so many Fords, and horses with the heads of lions breathing fire. I ate a small book that, I assure you, was as sweet as honey. I saw a lady *enceinte* who had twelve stars in her hair, and a red dragon with ten horns and seven lovely crowns on his head. I saw a woman who had the wings of an eagle, and a leopard with the feet of a cinnamon bear. I saw someone sitting on a cloud wielding a sickle. I saw three frogs jump out of a man's mouth, and a long sword come out of the mouth of another man. I saw a tree that bore twelve different kinds of fruit, and an animal with a man's face full of eyes back and front . . .

Drunk again? Not at all. I simply quote from the Bible.

III. ATTITUDE TOWARD POLITICS

§ 1

When I am charged with not taking a sufficiently serious interest in politics, in the doings of the crowd of low thieves and mountebanks down at Washington—a parcel of men almost wholly devoid of truth, decency and honor—it is precisely as if I were asked to take a serious interest in the doings of a union of piano-movers over in Long Island City. I decline to pollute my mind with such obscenities. Even the consideration of politics as a species of buffoonery does not hold any enchantment for me. I can see nothing enjoyable in riding on the steam cars for several days to look at a thousand dudelsocks who believe that the way to pick out the best man for President of the United States is to rip off their undershirts, tote around banners labeled "Oh You Kid!", sing "Ach, Du Lieber Augustin", squirt tobacco juice on the chairs, and periodically yell "Three cheers for Kansas!" Compared with such a spectacle, a Broadway leg-show is a master-

32

piece of diversion. I would rather look at a pretty leg once than at Barney Baruch twice—any day. And I would rather listen to a sightly wench warbling "Kiss Me on the Ear, Gus, My Mouth is Full of Gum" than to a suffragette chromo reciting the virtues of William G. McAdoo.

I am told that my complete disinterestedness in politics causes me to miss a lot. What do I miss? I miss a lot of imbecile statements mouthed by a lot of blockheads in behalf of a candidate who is generally a lot more of a blockhead than they are. I miss reading a lot of tripe about a lot of fourth-rate micks busying themselves with the noble enterprise of getting a third-rate job for a second-rate mick. I miss seeing democracy behind the scenes in its dressing-room, clad only in its chemise. I have no taste for such vulgarity. I prefer a good dog fight, or a burlesque show. The spectacle of a United States senator in the lavatory at a national convention, pickled to the ears and making an indignant speech on the League of Nations to three patriotic American delegates named, respectively, Winckheimer, Eiersalat and Schnitzblauser, or of a candidate for the Presidency, boiled to the eyebrows, trying to make an impression on the newspaper correspondents, grabbing the edge of a table to steady himself and, missing it, landing plumb on his *Sitzfleisch*

33

—such spectacles are only a cheap imitation of Robie's Crackerjack Burlesquers. And I prefer to get such a show at first hand. Why travel for days at the cost of hundreds of dollars to see something that I can see done much better down in Fourteenth Street for seventy-five cents? The clowns of politics are no whit more real than the clowns of the stage: a senator, or even a President, and Herman Krausmeyer are brothers under their skin; both are equally mummers. The slapstick that lands to the rear of a politician, however eminent, and the one that lands to the rear of a stage pantaloon are, to me, one and the same, and the respective seats upon which the slapsticks land are no less one and the same. And when it is argued that politics provides the greater and lewder show because in the theatre one has to pretend that the slapstické is someone of dignity and consequence in order properly to appreciate the humors of his embarrassment consequent upon the receipt of the wallop, I argue in turn that one has to pretend exactly the same thing in the case of politics. Thus, if in the pursuit of ribald jocosity I have to imagine for the time being that some burlesque show ham is the Count de Roquefort, owner of the Deauville Casino, the lover of politics in turn has to imagine that some erstwhile shyster lawyer from Sandusky, Ohio, or Kraus Creek, Minnesota,

is a purple toga'd Mark Antony with a liberal
soupçon of Roman in him. The buffoons of
politics, in good truth, are less real than the buffoons of the stage. Which, for example, is the
more convincing: William H. Crane's United
States senator or J. Thomas Heflin's? If the
essence of humor lies in the sharp contrast between
dignity and importance on the one hand and
sudden disaster and ignominy on the other, one
may inquire as to the dignity and importance of
the politician. That dignity and importance exist
simply in the mind of the spectator, through a
voluntary remission of judgment, exactly as in the
case of the stage actor. If, in order to pave the
way for a good loud belly-laugh, I have to pretend
to myself that Louis Mann, say, is a millionaire
steel magnate, a lover of rare books and a powerful thinker, the devotee of politics has to pretend
to himself that a United States ambassador to a
great European capital is a sagacious statesman
and diplomat, and not—as he more often actually
is—merely an American who can wear a silk hat
without looking like a French hack driver, who can
stand on a polished hard-wood floor without slip-
ping, and who has learned how to say "This soup
is delicious" in two foreign languages.

As it is pretty well agreed, even by the most
enthusiastic followers of political phenomena, that

about ninety-five per cent of politicians are idiots,
I cannot quite grasp the pleasure that these followers derive from watching them swell up and
explode. In Matteawan perhaps ninety-five per
cent of the incarcerated idiots imagine themselves
to be senators, ambassadors, governors and even
Presidents. I might thus get the same degree of
amusement contemplating these poor fellows as I
can get contemplating those of their brothers who
are still at large. The circumstance that a politician is gravely accepted by three or four hundred
thousand dinkelspiels for the sage he pretends to
be, and that he deceives himself in the same direction, surely does not make him any better material
for a cultivated man's risibilities than a mere stage
anticker. There were just as many dolts who
believed that Richard Mansfield was a great intellectual and great art force as there were dolts who
believed that Woodrow Wilson was a Gladstone
and Bismarck. The mob may regard a Governor
of Tennessee as a more important man than Cabell,
or Borglum, or even Bach, but the same mob in
turn regards Charlie Chaplin as a more important
man than a Governor of Tennessee—and I am not
certain that, here at least, the mob isn't partly
right. Carrying out to its logical conclusion the
contention that the humor of politics lies entirely

in the accepted eminence of politicians and the consequent relatively more emphatic report that issues from the collision of their seats with the pavement, it might be said that Elihu Root, whom hundreds of thousands of Americans soberly consider a Socrates, is by that fact, and that fact solely, a droller dill-pickle than Al Jolson, whom the same number of Americans frankly consider a clown. Therefore, in conclusion, I fear that it would be silly for me to waste years trying to acquire a talent for laughing at politicians. The thing would be just as insane as for Beethoven to have given up music and to have devoted ten or twenty years to learning how to paint on china.

§ 2

If Christ came to Chicago, He wouldn't be one-tenth so flabbergasted as would George Washington were he to come to Washington, D. C.

§ 3

A President of the United States must ever be the target of intelligent ridicule and criticism, not to mention a secondary fusillade of bean-shooters, custard pies and asafœtida bombs. God never made a man who could set himself up as a leader of 100,000,000 people without coincidently setting himself up as something of an unconscious, vain hanswurst.

§ 4

Politics is a peep-show the particular low humor of which is derived from the circumstance that the performers have their eyes glued to the other end of the same keyhole that is used by the onlooking customers.

§ 5

The technic of democratic government is to impose responsibility upon the shoulders of the irresponsible. The technic of monarchical government is aristocratically to reserve irresponsibility for the responsible.

§ 6

Politics is the refuge of scoundrels—from other scoundrels.

§ 7

Does it occur to those republican Frenchmen who protest against the election of a professional soldier as first president of the German republic that the first president of their own republic after

the Commune was similarly a professional soldier? Does it occur to those super-republican
Americanos who, following the French, bawl
against the election of a military leader as first
president of the German republic that the first
president of their own republic was just such a
military leader?

§ 8

Democracy is the form of government that
places responsibility upon the man who believes
that if he gives a check to his bootlegger made
out to "Cash" instead of to "Bearer", the prohibition spies won't be able to trace the purchase of
the schnapps to him.

§ 9

It is no longer the habit of our Presidents to
kiss babies. Babies, they have learned, sometimes
tell.

§ 10

The late war was fought to make the world safe
for democracy. The ensuing peace has been
fought to make democracy unsafe for Russia and
Germany.

§ 11

A Socialist is ideally fitted for going to jail. All his ideas are ready-made and quite solid, and so he can risk being alone. Unlike other men, solitude brings him no metaphysical and philosophical doubts, concerns and despairs. Socialism is thus a sort of insurance against insanity, like patriotism and religion. A man swallows it, gives up thinking, and is happy.

§ 12

Perfect democracy is possible only in a royal household.

§ 13

"God", said Napoleon, "is on the side of the heaviest battalions". But that was yesterday. Today, God is on the side of the shrewdest diplomats.

§ 14

The voice of the people is the voice of God. Therefore, the *Congressional Record* is the Bible.

IV. ATTITUDE TOWARD HOMO SAPIENS

§ 1

A man's tastes, in essence, change little. His tastes at fifty are at bottom his tastes of twenty filtered through the gauze of wisdom, prudence and ennui.

§ 2

Every man is a hedonist. The only difference between the two varieties of the sons of Aristippus is that one hedonist seeks his goal of pleasure on earth and that the other seeks his in heaven. The latter, posturing his anti-Cyrenaic doctrine, is actually the more selfish and more positively hedonistic of the two, since where the former seeks only the transitory and impermanent pleasures that the earth and his days upon it can vouchsafe him, the other seeks instead, under the gaudy labels of altruism, idealism, etc., with which he self-deceptively plasters himself, the everlasting and immutable pleasures of the world hereafter.

41

§ 3

The happiest time of a man's life is not, as has been said, when his illusions have gone completely, but rather when his illusions are just beginning to scoot around the corner.

§ 4

A man's conscience is usually so cowardly that it is afraid even of him, and so it doesn't bother him much—and his memories and spiritual kidneys cloud and clot as the years go plunging by.

§ 5

Companionship is a matter of mutual weaknesses. We like that man or woman best who has the same faults that we have.

§ 6

I should like to have a son—provided there were some way of his being born into the world at the age of fifteen. The thought of the previous years of my potential son has kept me from making my wish concrete, for up to the age of fifteen he would be of little interest to me: I can presently get the same comfort and amusement from a good dog. But if I could have a son of fifteen years, as other men have sons of fifteen seconds, I should call up the nearest bishop and have him marry me to the first pretty girl (white) who walked past the church. There must be considerable fun and satisfaction to be had from such a son. He is at fifteen just beginning to get on his legs, so to speak, and to comprehend in a relative manner and degree the world into which he has come. Before fifteen, the clay is still too soft and sticky; one cannot work with it. But the boy of fifteen is already taking form. His steps may be directed; his mind may be approached; his heart may be cultivated. His longing for all-day peppermint suckers, the making of mudpies and the Presidency of the United States has, with the first faint dawn of intelligence, left him, and he is ready for better things, for nobler and finer ambitions. He has ceased to be a mere living and breathing jumping-jack wherewith to divert one's self after the day's chores are done and has become something approaching to a man. I should like to have a son like that without the otherwise inevitable and nuisanceful preliminaries of diapers, wet nurses, christening ceremonies, chicken pox and breaking of the neighbors' windows. The conversation of a boy of fifteen is more amusing than that of the majority of the young women upon whom, under present conditions and circumstances, I rely for relaxation, and the inborn admiration of a son for his father—however balmy the latter—would be eminently satisfying to my ego. The most interesting period in a boy's life is from fifteen to twenty-one. I should, I repeat, like to have a son in those years. Before fifteen, I'd rent him out to the movies. After twenty-one—if I have learned anything of the wisdom of the world—I'd shoot him.

§ 7

There is a type of man who, consciously possessed of an inferior mind, seeks to make himself effective in a conversation by resorting to contradictions. In contradicting his superiors he achieves for himself the little moments of self-importance and personal reassurance that in straightforward, honest and intelligent argument would be wholly beyond his reach.

§ 8

One of the greatest of all bores is the precisionist in the use of words, the kind of person who in conversation is meticulously concerned with the exact use of the English language. Scrupulous English is the murderer of interesting colloquy. Conversation under such circumstances becomes less verbal intercourse between two human beings than a contest between two etymologists and grammarians.

§ 9

What is called dignity is a subterfuge wherewith second-rate men seek to conceal their deficiencies.

§ 10

Nothing is more offensive to me than the affability toward me of men for whom I have no respect.

§ 11

Every man should specify in a codicil to his last will and testament that under no circumstances are his letters, to whomsoever written during his lifetime, to be published after his death. The only conceivable exceptions should be such vain fellows, of whom there are a few, as deliberately compose letters with an eye to their posthumous publication. These letters, of course, are not actually letters at all, but purposeful literary documents—posturing, insincere, and of the popinjay all compact. They are no more letters, properly speaking, than Grant's Tomb is a deviled ham sandwich. The letters written by other men are, however and nevertheless, generally equally unrevelatory so far as the men themselves are concerned. And where they do reveal the character and nature of their writers, they usually have so little claim to literary value, or any other sound value, that their publication disgraces the respective corpses. A man may tell the truth about himself and his acquaintances in a few letters during his life-time, but the letters he customarily writes illuminate him with a very dim honesty. For once that he tells the truth about the way some man has swindled him, he fails ten times to tell the truth about the ways he, in turn, swindled other men. For once he writes a letter saying what he actually thinks, he twenty times writes letters saying merely what he knows will please the recipients of those letters. A man's letters, in short, represent less himself than more or less necessary evasions of himself.

Even in the doodlish department of love-letter writing, a man's epistolary confections seldom have much sincerity. Where sincerity creeps in to any considerable degree, the love-letter descends very largely to rubber-stamp expressions and terms of endearment as old as John the Baptist, and so is not worth publishing. A man generally writes his love-letters, if he compromises his dignity so far as to write them at all, not for their truth, but for their sound—and they hence give us very much less accurate news of his character and nature than, say, his laundry bills. Now and again a poet's love-letters are worth publication, yet this is not because they are letters, but because they are literary compositions converted into letters only by the grace of a postage stamp and the circumstance that some post-office clerk has canceled it with some such message as "Don't Forget Ashtabula Old-Home Week".

§ 12

Children, as they grow older and come to know the world, peculiarly reserve their greater admiration and love for that one of their parents whose life was corrupted by weaknesses and who, in the pathos of distance, thus appears to them a more charming and wistful figure than the other and nobler parent.

§ 13

Nothing grows tiresome so quickly as an interesting talker.

§ 14

Where you find a log-roller you find, relevantly and simultaneously, a wooden-head.

§ 15

I distrust the geniality of fat men.

47

§ 16

I have never had a good friend, nor do I care ever to have one, who was not, or will not be, possessed of a considerable measure of vanity. I admire men who have reason for vanity, and are at no pains to conceal it.

§ 17

It has been said that whenever a man encounters a woman in a mood he doesn't understand, he wants to know if she is tired. Similarly, when a man encounters a woman who is sad, he invariably believes that her sadness can only have some association with love.

§ 18

Every man over the age of forty should put aside a certain amount of money each year for use as a nonsense fund. It is a rare man, and a liar, who will not confess to the possession of certain occasional idiotic sprees of fancy which he is unable to gratify. The regular and constant suppression of such wish-jags makes in time for a measure of unhappiness, an unhappiness which, though fundamentally trivial, colors the man's days and life and philosophy. The wish-jags of

every man need release, and this release they may
find only through such a fund as I have indicated.
The amount set aside for these annual sailor's
debauches of the wish-complex need not be large
in the instance of the majority of men, for the
majority of men's absurd wishes are in the main
of a not very considerable bulk. They take
some such form as a five dollar necktie or a dollar and a quarter cigar or a bottle of Charente
brandy. But, though they are not great, a man's
failure to realize them gets to him, as the
phrase has it, and contrives to lodge a fly in the
ointment of his mood. The man knows that
he can afford to buy the things, but that is not
the point. He does not buy them, or anything else
of the kind upon which his foolish fancy has
alighted, for the simple reason that they seem a bit
too extravagant and unnecessary. A nonsense
fund would take care of such things and make the
average fellow happy. It would be a fund for
him to squander with a grandiose nonchalance; it
would not figure in his strict finances; it would be
viewed by him in the light of found money or
money won on a bet or inherited from a forgotten
uncle. With it he might buy that case of Clicquot
Ponsardin 1911, or that green vest, or that gilt
piano upon which he has long rested a longing and
frustrated eye.

49

§ 19

The most delightful of companions is he who combines the mind of a gentleman with the emotions of a bum.

§ 20

Some boys go to college and eventually succeed in getting out. Others go to college and never succeed in getting out. The latter are called professors.

§ 21

It is only strong men who suffer pain from petty tragedies.

§ 22

It is the most puzzling of human paradoxes that one often feels the most spiritually depressed in the moments of one's highest material happiness.

§ 23

The infelicity and charming muddle-headedness with which the average man selects a woman for the object of his affections may readily be appreciated through the application of a simple test. Say that this same man were commissioned with the duty of selecting a woman for his best, most valued and most respected friend. Would he for a moment think of selecting for this esteemed friend the woman whom he has selected for himself? Would he not rather search for a woman possessed of many of the very qualities in which his own inamorata is lacking? Would he not select a woman in many respects the very opposite of his own choice? I leave the answer to you and to your own experience.

§ 24

The worth-while man generally has a streak of laziness in him. It is the essentially snide fellow who is ever on the alert, ever up-and-doing, ever the consistent go-getter. Vigor is an overestimated quality. Much of the greatest and most dramatic work in the world has been done by men who have been just a bit tired.

§ 25

There is one thing, at least, that age is not successful in deceiving itself about. It may lie convincingly to itself about a hundred different things, but it stubs its toe embarrassingly when it is met with an invitation to toboggan. A man and woman become definitely old in their own consciousness the moment the toboggan sled begins to seem risky and uninviting to them.

§ 26

Only ignorant persons seek intelligence in their companions after dark.

§ 27

One regards the man who makes a witty retort as a delightful fellow. But one regards the man who makes two witty retorts as something of a bore.

§ 28

My friends, no less than I, have their peculiarities. One of them, for example, carries an umbrella even on fair days in the fond belief that it makes him look English. Another is in the habit constantly of bearing himself erect as a poker in the fond belief that it makes him look dignified and important. Still another speaks in terms of light and easy derogation of all the well-known and important persons he is acquainted with in the fond belief that it makes him seem unaffected and pleasantly democratic and of independent judgment. Another still has a habit of growling into the telephone when he lifts off the receiver and

then becoming instantly suave and amiable again
by way of leading persons at the other end to believe that while he doesn't like most of the persons
who call him up he does like them. And a fifth
generally seeks to confound an unanswerable argument by employing soft, velvet tones in his replies
to a somewhat vociferous opponent. . . .

§ 29

The notion that every boy is a great admirer
of his father is not strictly true. What is true is
that every boy is a great bragger about his father
to the neighbor's boy, and vice versa. Neither of
them believes the half of it.

§ 30

A man changes every seven years of his life.
A woman changes but once in her life.

§ 31

Portrait of a Man.—He is my friend. He fa-
vors bloody wars in which hundreds of thousands
meet their death, and collects cigar-bands for his
little four-year-old niece. He is a champion of
the Nietzschean doctrine, and spends considerable
time each year in Schwartz's toy store picking out
doll babies and choo-choo cars for the youngsters

53

of his married acquaintances. He has above his writing table a large framed photograph of the Iron Chancellor, and on his writing table a small framed photograph of a very pretty girl. He chews tobacco, and his favorite musical compositions are the waltzes of Johann Strauss. He is a foe of democracy, and politely sees every person, however asinine, who comes to call on him. He believes and stoutly maintains that one strong enemy is more valuable than two mediocre friends, and then makes friends with the strong enemy soon after he shows up. He is in favor of a merciless autocracy, and collects postage stamps for his brother's little child. He is a rabid anti-Prohibitionist and gets a violent attack of heartburn and a sour middle whenever he drinks two cocktails. He scorns society, but has his evening clothes made by one of the best and most expensive of Fifth Avenue tailors. He lustily derides golf players, and amuses himself for a couple of hours every afternoon playing with some pet turtles in his back-yard. He champions Germany and the Germans to the full power of his talents, and runs a block to keep from meeting the average German who wishes an audience with him. He writes vehemently against quack doctors, and has tried ten of them in an attempt to get rid of his hay-fever. He insists that he likes only the company of middle-aged women, and associates solely with young ones. He ridicules any man who is vain in the matter of personal appearance, and goes out and buys a new necktie if the ones he has with him do not match the shirt he is wearing. He is an exponent of the "Be hard" doctrine, is in favor of killing off the weak, and sends milk twice a month to the starving babies of the war-ridden European countries. He is a fatalist, and doses himself daily with a half dozen various philtres. . . .

§ 32

The most pitiable of all human emotions is the gayety of despair.

§ 33

A man begins to grow definitely old on that day when first he begins to admire old-fashioned girls.

§ 34

A fool is one who is intelligent at the wrong time.

§ 35

Let us not overlook the fact, too, that all millionaires are members of the hated and much criticized minority.

§ 36

It is not man's tragedy that his body grows old, but that his mind does. The arteries of happiness inevitably harden with the years. Wisdom and experience never yet have brought back the happiness of youth.

§ 37

When a man looks at a photograph of himself as a little boy, he sees there less himself than one who seems his own child.

§ 38

Motoring through the country a short time ago, I saw a cow gazing amorously at the bull on a Bull Durham billboard. In that cow's eyes lay, as I have never seen it so illuminatingly expressed, the philosophy of the futility of most men's earthly longings, ambitions and dreams.

§ 39

Toward men, ever an aristocrat; toward women, ever a commoner—that way lies success.

§ 40

Much sentimental mush is written about a man's first sweetheart. Take, for example, your own case. Try, if you will, to think of her name! A man's first sweetheart is generally less a subject for the poets than for Havelock Ellis.

§ 41

The young man and the old man seek pretty women. The man of middle years finds his greatest enjoyment in the company of women who are comparatively plain. Unlike the young man and the old man he is in that period of his life where he does not wish to exert himself and the comparatively plain woman offers him much less of the customary resistance of a pretty woman's vanity. The young man takes pride in conquering the challenge of that vanity. The old man, a dodo in vanity on his own, seeks to recapture his youth in similarly taking up the challenge. The middle-aged man is between the two poles. What he wants, and wants above everything in women, is a charming, engaging and romantically warming comfort.

§ 42

I have yet to attend a great social affair at which all the most eligible bachelors present were not trying to break away to keep a date with some comparative Cinderella.

§ 43

In all the numerous fields of human ingenuity and enterprise, none shows so small a measure of progress as that which concerns itself with the artificial thatching of the male mammal's bald dome. Human imagination and skill have triumphed over fire and water, the air and the land, the sea and the jungle; they have chained electricity and water falls; they have defied the flight of birds and the very passing of time. But the wig in this Year of Our Lord 1925 is still the melancholy looking and completely obvious dingus that it was in the Sixteenth Century. It is reasonable to believe that thousands upon thousands of men in the last five or six centuries, and particularly in the last, have labored to perfect a wig that would be at least partly deceptive, that would seem to belong where it was put. And yet with what result? With the result that the wig looks today exactly like—a wig.

There never has been a wig or a toupé that could deceive even an onlooker with a violent case of astigmatism. One can spot the spurious covering on a bald head a block away. It is approximately as successful in concealing the fact that a man hasn't any of his own hair left as a bustle is successful in concealing the fact that a woman is deficient in what need not further be described.

The wig or the toupé, in fact, does not so much conceal baldness as loudly announce it. The only person it fools is the man who wears it. Yet why should this be? Why should one of the apparently most simple things in the world thus baffle human ingenuity?

§ 44

Nothing is so ruinous to the success of a dinner party as good food.

§ 45

It is a fact of history that, since the beginning of the Christian era, there have been only two men possessed of noteworthy imagination who have been content to love but one woman in their lives.

§ 46

It has been my experience to find that men who seek intelligence in their companions among the fair sex are men whose friends, cronies and companions among the sterner sex are wanting in intelligence. When one finds a man who admires women in proportion as they are intelligent, one finds synchronously a man whose men friends, due to his limited acquaintance, his lack of contact with the intellectual world or his personal defi-

59

ciency in persuading interesting men to gather about him, are dull fellows and profound bores.

§ 47

A man's underwear symbolizes his view of himself. It constitutes an intimate and secret self-estimate. What he puts next to his epidermis reveals his private notion of his just deserts.

§ 48

One of the most beautiful of all things is a beautiful lamp. Nothing in the world, save it be music, can so soothe and set adream the mood of mortal man. The past and all the present and some of the future are encompassed in its soft, persuasive glow. It is the symbol of love, of home, of wistful and vagrant fancy, of all the hopes and despairs of one's life on earth. God made the sun and moon and stars, but man, His child, out of necessity made for himself the lamplight as a beacon and a haven for the innermost secrets of his heart of hearts.

§ 49

I am always skeptical of the honesty of a man's culture if his library shelves fail to reveal at least a few grotesquely unintelligible volumes. In the heart of every genuinely cultivated man there is a peculiar fondness for certain books that, though perhaps trashy and empty to some of us, are for one reason or another close to his secret fancy.

§ 50

There is no affair so stupid as that presided over by a too jolly host.

§ 51

Anything beyond two ash-carts and an ice-wagon looks like a circus parade to a man who has lived all his life in a small town.

§ 52

The man of honor tells the truth to men and lies to women. The man of dishonor tells the truth to women and lies to men.

§ 53

The inferior man's hatred of his superior often takes the form of being humorous at the latter's expense. A bitter heart is frequently the cradle of a biting wit. Men cry for their slaves and laugh at their masters.

61

§ 54

Happiness is ruinous to accomplishment. Few men can do first-rate work when they are bathed in a mood of expansive cheer. A touch of unhappiness, of concern, of discontent, is essential to vigorous enterprise and achievement. When everything is going with beautiful smoothness in a man's daily life, his work immediately shows the effects of it. He slacks up a trifle; he takes a bit too much for granted; he slides back, however imperceptibly. It is when things are not exactly hotsy-totsy with him that he produces the best that there is in him. No man ever accomplished anything on the day he counted up his first thousand dollars, or on the day before he was to make his first trip to Munich, or on the day his forgotten uncle died in Australia and left him his estates, or on the day he paid down the last instalment on his electric piano, or on the day he got married. Napoleon's happiness at Ligny caught him by the throat a few days later at Waterloo. Haydn lost his lady love to a convent and, married in despair to her elder homely sister, wrote his masterpieces with a broken heart. George F. Babbitt himself shone with particular lustre in the realtor field only when the world and the devil had sardonically at him.

§ 55

Not a month passes that I don't do something that makes me seem a fool in my own eyes and makes me want to take myself out into the street and kick myself around the block. That I don't do so is due to the consolation I find in the fact that most other men are donkeys just as often as I am. On the occasions when I make a spectacle of myself, I therefore woo back my self-esteem simply by looking around me at my brothers in dunderhead-edness and by comfortably recalling what a fool every man, past or present, who has my highest respect has periodically made of himself.

§ 56

Like most other men, I have been the recipient of thousands of pieces of advice during my life-time. All of them save two I have found utterly worthless. The two were: *1.* Never eat corned beef and cabbage and ice-cream at the same meal; and *2.* Pulling down the eyelid and blowing the nose has not succeeded in getting a cinder out of one's eye since 416 B. C.

V. ATTITUDE TOWARD GYNEOLATRY

§ 1

One may tell the truth with impunity only to very pretty women.

§ 2

In every thoroughly charming and effective person, one finds a suggestion and trace, however small, of the gutter. This trace of finished vulgarity is essential to a completely winning manner. The suavest and most highly polished man or woman becomes uninteresting save he or she possess it. In the soul of every fetching man, there is a streak of ingratiating commonness; in the heart of every alluring silken woman, there is a touch of calico.

§ 3

There is only in the rarest of cases such a thing as loyalty in women. A man will remain loyal to an ideal even where he finds that it is no longer an ideal; a woman remains loyal only so long as the object of her loyalty, whatever it may be, remains fixed and stable. And even then her loyalty is at times cast o'er with doubt.

§ 4

It is seldom that the beauty of a woman's face can survive her laughter.

§ 5

The letter of a woman is always more honest and more sincere than the letter of a man. A woman writes what she thinks and feels at the moment; a man, what he thinks he may think and feel tomorrow in terms of what he thought and felt yesterday.

§ 6

Why admire intelligence in a beautiful woman? Does one ask that a Turner landscape be intelligent? Does one itch to have a song by Brahms stimulate one's thoughts to speculations on basal metabolism, the theory of relativity, or the elimination of urticaria following injections of horse-serum? Simple beauty should be enough for any man, not himself a blockhead. Woman, as I see her, is a spectacle, not a chautauqua. Intelligence

65

ruins a pretty woman, as intelligence ruins a pretty lyric.

There are men, to the contrary, who, seeking recreation in women, fail to find that recreation unless their vis-à-vis be possessed of sagacity. Beauty is not enough for them. Yet what can be more recreative than beauty as beauty? Do they need a woman to hold their hands when their eyes are regaled by the beauty of the Austrian Tyrol, or by the Champs Elysées in the Spring when the yellow night-lights are on, or by a long blue-white stretch of sea and sand? Can they not find a greater companionship in this beauty than in any intelligent woman they ever met, and bought a bad dinner for? To look at a woman through one's ears, as men who seek intelligence in women look, is like looking at perfume or smelling music.

§ 7

There are men whose delight in women is not chiefly visual, as mine happens to be, but aural. Show them any woman who has a low and musical voice and promptly they are fetched by her. Blindfold such fellows and they would believe my colored charwoman to be the loveliest creature in the United States.

§ 8

It has been my experience that tall women are generally dull conversationalists.

§ 9

Nothing quite so ruins the effect of a woman's prettiness and charm as a mood of emphasis. The most beautiful and attractive of women loses much of her beauty and attractiveness when she becomes emphatic. When emphasis enters a woman's mouth, fascination coincidently makes its getaway.

§ 10

The contention that, so far as a man is concerned, the pleasantest of all parties is the twosome, that is, one composed of a fellow and a girl who like each other, is no longer maintained save by professors of the orthodox and banal. The true masculine gourmet of pleasure knows from long experience that the most amusing party ever devised by the angels on high is the one that is made up of one man and two girls, and that its amusement qualities are not much interfered with one way or the other whether the attendants like one another or not. In point of fact, the less they like one another the more likely the party is to be to the taste of the man, assuming him, of course, to be a member of what may be called cultured society.

The twosome generally repeats itself. One such party is as much like another as the soup stains on a congressman's waistcoat. The man who can still find gratification of the spirit in sitting around with a girl, holding her hand under the table, gazing lovingly at her ear and whispering sweet emptinesses to her is either a recent college graduate, who hence knows nothing, or a vain old idiot of a bachelor making a gallant and futile stab at youth and romance. The man of any intelligence who spends an evening at a table with a fair creature may, true enough, enjoy the first half-hour, but he is a fraud who would seriously maintain that thereafter the party does not descend to the time-worn stencils and rubber-stamps. Recall, if you will, that it is the amusement-power of such parties of which I am speaking—nothing else. And with this in mind, consider the relative pleasure to be derived from the triangular party: the one composed of one man and two girls. Here is humor in its fullest promise! Where, in the case of one man and one girl, both the man and the girl feel a certain amount of reserve, and conduct themselves accordingly, this reserve, as everyone knows, promptly disappears when an extra girl is on the scene, and to the establishment of the necessary gala note. What one girl will talk about with a man isn't worth listening to, save perhaps by young boys and adult mushheads. But what *two* girls will talk about with a man is worthy the attention of the savant! No man who has experienced the joys of the mixed threesome will for a moment debate its tremendously superior humorous horsepower. The conversation at such a *grand concert apéritif* has life, salt, gayety, wit, searching truth, and the charm that lies ever in the heart of frankness. The conversation at the party made up of a fellow and a girl is usually fit only for the ears of imbeciles, already full-blown or potential.

§ 11

A woman will stop at nothing, including marriage, to convince herself that she is no longer in love with the man she is in love with.

§ 12

Lucky the woman who can conceal her greatest and most secret defect from her rival!

69

§ 13

Life is full of surprises. But not to a woman over twenty-five or a man over thirty.

§ 14

A man, winning the favor of the woman of his choice, congratulates himself on the success of his technic, the while the woman, who has already made up her mind long before the aforesaid technic ever got into action, sits back and quietly treats herself to a low snicker.

§ 15

Although so great a philosopher as Nietzsche defined woman as a plaything—"the reward of the warrior" was his phrase—any lesser man who would repeat the definition today would be set down as an impresario of gibberish. Now that old Friedrich is dead, it is apparently permitted to Frenchmen alone to write of women with any degree of honesty. The Anglo-Saxon and certain others deem it proper to speak of the ladies only in tones customarily reserved for the Deity; to be a trifle realistic in the philosophic contemplation of them, they regard as not quite nice. Yet, unless I am submerged in error, woman is and always has been primarily a plaything. She herself may at times and in certain instances try to blink the fact—particularly when she happens to be so unprepossessing that no man wants her for a plaything—but in her heart of hearts she knows the truth of it. Of this truth, a certain increasingly prevalent sexual phenomenon among women offers illuminating evidence. This phenomenon is, in essence, nothing but a challenge and a resentment.

The by this time already irritated reader will have observed that I generalize about women. He will object to this generalization. But, since it is I and not he who is writing this, the generalization must stand. Generalizations are not always faulty. One may generalize with a fair degree of accuracy on numerous subjects. War is one of them. Hygiene is another. Sculpture and bock beer are still others. And woman is, I believe, another still. The men who group women under certain different classifications marry them. And, as Omnipotence has willed it, I happen to be a bachelor. I am not unduly swollen over the fact; I offer it to the jury, indeed, as evidence against myself. I simply remain still to be convinced. Toward the aforesaid conviction, I have at times drifted, but the old tugboat has somehow ever remained in midstream. And there, for the time being, it remains rolling *a cappella* at anchor.

It is, to get back on the key, foolish to group women under various headings. Only men may be so grouped. Men differ, in many essentials. But all women are, at bottom, much the same. The O'Grady and the Colonel's lady, up to the age of thirty-five at least, are sisters under their skins. But do not mistake me, please. I do not pose as a Ph.D. of the fair sex. I simply set down the results of my own observation. If these results collide with your own, then one of us is wrong. It may be I; but it may too, on the other hand, be you. Woman, it seems to me, was wrought primarily by an all-wise Creator for man's entertainment and bemusement. That she is the mother of the race hardly invalidates the point. The moment a man's wife no longer amuses him—I use the word "amuse", obviously enough, in its broadest sense—he grows sick of her and she too, by the act of droll and ironic fate, grows tired of him. The best mother is she who seems to her little son her father's delicate and beautiful sweetheart. No son of a raucous suffragette admires his mother as the son of a sweet and amiable woman does his. A boy in his youngsterhood plays with girls. And, save he be an absurd sentimentalist and an out-and-out emotional Babbitt when he grows up, he continues to do so until he dies. That he may marry offers no argument against this point of view. Ninety-nine men out of a hundred look on their wives as playthings when they marry them, for love is a music written for playthings. When they stop regarding their wives as playthings, they no longer love them with the quality of love that launched their marriage. The woman then loses much of her femininity in the husband's eyes and gains a touch of quasi-masculinity. She becomes, in a word, his partner in the dull business routine of life. He admires her; he respects her; but he no longer loves her in the sense that he originally loved her—and it is that original love that every wife pines for. The heart of a woman, whatever her age and however wrinkled her face, remains always the heart of a girl.

I have known many women in this life of mine and, among them all, I have never known one who did not, in the lovely heart of her, wish to be, above all the more serious things of the world, a pretty and desirable toy. A woman is always a plaything for the man she truly loves. It is only when she does not truly love that she takes on a coat of another color. The man who is married to a woman who is not a plaything is married to a woman who may venerate him and be loyal to him but who doesn't really love him. . . . Almost every woman is a plaything on her honeymoon. It is in the years that follow—years often disillusionizing to her—

that she changes and ceases to be. She perhaps wishes still to be a plaything, but she no longer has the right playmate. For one can't be a plaything when illusion has gone its way. It is thus that married women so frequently seek innocent unction to their vanity in the company of men other than their husbands. The old longing to be regarded as a plaything tugs at their bosoms; they want to hear the light-hearted old phrases and see the light-hearted old smiles, long since forgotten by the men to whom they are wedded. . . . Every time a woman buys a new dress or puts on a new hat, it is of herself as a plaything that she is thinking. Thinking—but never under any circumstance so analyzing herself. For once she tries to define it, the plaything spirit is already, so far as she is concerned, on its death-bed calling weakly for the hot-water bottle. The moment a woman begins to analyze herself as a plaything, she ceases to be one. A toy doesn't think.

Why is it that the women of the stage are generally more alluring than the women in private life? Because they have about them the plaything air. Has it been woman as woman or woman as plaything that has ruled kings and emperors and the great generals of the world? Is the library of romance full of the stories of women who haven't been playthings or of women who have been?

For one woman who wins a man by other means, there are a score who win by their toy quality. . . . I have said that, in her heart, every woman wishes to be a plaything. There are interludes in this wish, of course. There are times when doubt and unhappiness and thoughts of tomorrow turn the light melody into a graver key. But, so long as a woman is immediately happy, so long does she enthusiastically concur in the plaything estimate of her.

I have, in the last two or three years, read no less than one hundred male-made articles in magazines and newspapers entitled "Why I Have Never Married". The gentlemen who have thus taken the public into their confidence are doubtless entirely honest and sincere, but the reasons they assign for never having married would be just as convincing if the articles were written by women. These reasons are generally found to be purely sentimental ones. This man has never married either because, so he says, he has never been able to find a girl like his mother or because the lady on whom he was excessively mashed was drowned five days before the wedding. And that man has never married, he confesses, because he deemed the building up of a shoe factory more important than the building up of a home or because the one girl in the whole world whom he would have mar-

ried gave him the gate. There are doubtless men
who have never married for such reasons, but they
are, I believe, few and far between. Though they
are, as I have observed, sincere and honest in setting down their personal records, they are, it seems
to me, the exception to the rule rather than the rule
itself. For one man who hasn't married because
he couldn't find a girl with the qualities of his
mother or because his first sweetmeat was run over
by a Ford, there are a half-dozen like myself who
haven't married simply because marriage doesn't
strike their realistic minds as being one-half so
attractive as bachelorhood.

These so-called cynical fellows are not, however, wholly unsentimental. The only difference
between them and the other fellows is that, while
they are perfectly willing occasionally to sentimentalize women, they cannot find it in themselves
to sentimentalize matrimony. At least, not so
long as they are still relatively young and comfortable and happy. To particularize, I have
never married because, very simply, in the language of a current music show ditty, I am having
too much fun. I can think of nothing that marriage could give me, but I can think of many things
it could take away from me. It could, for example, take away from me the freedom I currently
enjoy in unloading into print any view on any

subject that comes into my head. If I were married—this being America—I should have to stop periodically and deliberate as to the tact of writing and printing certain ideas which presently I may freely deliver myself of. A married man must ever be more or less conscious of what people will think of him; there is his wife to be thought of in her relation to him and to his position in their immediate community. A bachelor knows no such hindrances. The married man who would write and publish such a treatise as this would find a rolling-pin waiting for him when he got home.

Marriage could take away my precious privacy, my present ability to go where I wish to whenever I wish to, my present agreeable habit of making even more agreeable engagements at the last moment and breaking less agreeable ones at the same time, my perfect equanimity of mind, my intense dislike of life insurance agents, and my freely voiced credo that there is always a slightly more charming young woman just around the corner. It could give me nothing otherwise that I, with the aid of six head of clairvoyants, am able to deduce. It is not that I shirk responsibility; it is that I shirk what I do not especially regard as responsibility. And connubial bliss is one of the responsibilities that I do not consider my own. The theory that it is the duty of every man to

77

marry strikes me as somewhat ridiculous. It may be the duty of every man of a certain kind to marry, but that is another matter. I personally have the misfortune to be unfitted temperamentally for hymeneal blessedness. I do not possess the required peculiar technic. That technic demands that a man spend the rest of his life with one woman and never look at another. Of this technic I am too much of an amateur. It is beyond me. And I am possessed of a strange and uncontrollable feeling that it is similarly beyond the majority of men who engage it. The manifold diversions that society devises for itself—dancing, drinking, racing, golf, European jaunts, charities, mah jong, and so on—are simply proofs of the constant failure of the technic in question and of the effort to forget that failure in opiates. These divertissements constitute, in essence, but a heroic resolve to make the well-mannered best of a bad bargain. I know many married men; I even know a few happily married men; but I don't know one who wouldn't fall down the first open coal-hole running after the first pretty girl who gave him a wink.

I appreciate that there are some fetching arguments in opposition to the general point of view herein exhibited, but none the less there seem to me to be some equally fetching arguments in support of it.   The mere circumstance that a point of view is an unpopular one does not confute it. Although the Anglo-Saxon places woman on a pedestal and the Latin does not, a French or Italian child loves its mother just as much as an English or American child does his.   I have always believed that, in fact, real and honest love flourishes best and most beautifully among such peoples as do not foolishly idealize women.

When I say that women are essentially playthings, I use the word not derogatorily but in terms of the highest compliment.   My mother was ever a charming and lovely pastime in my father's eyes.   My brother and I knew it, and we admired his attitude and loved her the more for it.   For we knew other fathers who looked on our boy friends' mothers with harder and prosier eyes, and we saw that these mothers of our boy friends showed it.   They scolded their sons, we noticed, a lot more and a lot oftener than our mother did us; and their smiles, we noticed, were sometimes sort of cold smiles where those of our mother seemed not to be.   We noticed these differences and many others, and if we then, as youngsters, didn't know the reason for them, that reason we began to know in our more mature and reflective years. . . . There is something infinitely alluring about a plaything.   The men who marry women who are not playthings marry for money, for position, for peace and comfort, for a multiplicity of reasons. But these have nothing to do with love. Where a man loves a woman really, you will generally find that the woman is, to him, above everything else the symbol of a boyhood toy. And so too will you frequently find that when a man hasn't married, it is simply because, while he may often have found the right kind of woman, he hasn't yet found the right kind of plaything.

§ 16

No woman can stand a sentimental man at the dinner table.

§ 17

I have never yet seen a woman who looked alluring when clothed in satin.

§ 18

Among men, women admire most those who have all the attributes and qualities of the actor and yet are not actors by profession.

§ 19

The most charming of women is she who remembers yesterday and forgets tomorrow.

§ 20

Married women whom one has known and been fond of in their single years seem always to be bent upon proving laboriously to one how happy they are.

§ 21

If you would succeed in society, tell married women you love them and single ones you don't.

§ 22

It is impossible for an imbecile to be a connoisseur of that imbecility of woman that is responsible for so much of her charm. Only an intelligent man can accurately and sympathetically appreciate such imbecility, as only a practised critic of literature can accurately and sympathetically appreciate the high art of such tomfoolery as George Ade's or Ring Lardner's. The ignoramus sees in a pretty moron only a pretty moron. The student sees in her the highest of all the feminine arts, the art of artlessness. That it is not a voluntary nor a consciously achieved art does not matter. Helen Green did not know that she was creating literature when she set down literally the imbecilities of imbecile telephone girls and vaudeville actors, nor did the ignoramuses

who read her. In the same way, many pretty
morons are, albeit indirectly, literary artists. Set
down their ignorance and imbecility literally on
paper, and it will be their ignorance and imbecility
that will be literature. The person who sets them
down will be merely the recorder. It will be their
own lack of ideas and lack of intelligence that will
produce the work of art. The raw materials and
the result will be one and the same thing.

§ 23

Woman is the holiday of man. Sometimes she
is the Christmas; sometimes she is the Valentine
day; sometimes she is the Labor Day; sometimes
she is the Decoration Day; more often she is the
Fourth of July.

§ 24

One's new girl is charming in the degree that her
charm differs from that of her predecessor.

§ 25

The yearning and desire for a child are naturally woman's. Such yearning and desire on
the part of a man, on the other hand, are indicative
of an essential feminine streak.

§ 26

No woman can be too beautiful and be a lady.

§ 27

A woman's most violent affection and passion are reserved for the first available man who crosses her path after she has lost the man she truly loves.

§ 28

Women, as they grow older, rely more and more on cosmetics. Men, as they grow older, rely more and more on a sense of humor.

§ 29

From "The Right Place", by the estimable C. E. Montague, I cull the following: "No one", said Fox, "could really be in love with Mrs. Siddons. Her scale, the huge structure of her genius, precluded any tender approach. In the court of love, as humanity knows it, her head would be sticking out through the roof. You might as well cherish a passion for Ursa Major or for the East India Company". Nicely put, we have here once again the sound platitude that men can't love women who are their superiors, or even their equals, in fame, in talent or in intelligence. Men love only their inferiors. If dogs could write fugues, men would promptly transfer their present affection for them to rats.

VI. ATTITUDE TOWARD PATRIOTISM

§ 1

What, precisely, is it that makes a man love his native land?   Is it his country's moral and ethical virtues?   Is it his country's strength and power? Is it his country's beauty, or glory, or splendor, or pride?   Is it any of these, or is it anything like these?   I doubt it.   The average man, 'way down deep in him, loves his country simply because it is more physically comfortable to him than any other, because, like an old pair of shoes, he is used to it, because its cooking suits his stomach better than the cooking of other countries, because he can't find a barber anywhere else as good as his home barber, and because its girls seem prettier to him than the girls of any other land.   A man is generally patriotic for much the same reason that he always wears the same kind of collar.

§ 2

One small piece of colored cheesecloth stuck on the end of a pole has often frustrated all the sober thinking that has been done since the world began.

§ 3

You will generally find that the man who howls most sardonically against patriotism is himself in essence a patriot. The only difference between him and the man he makes mock of is one of geographical scale. He himself may not love and whoop up his country, but if you say anything against his home town he will nine times out of ten rush eloquently to its defence.

§ 4

When armies, victorious or vanquished, return home after great and excessively bloody wars, one observes that the generals are never missing from the parades.

§ 5

It is a great American patriot who is still a patriot after listening to the smoking-room conversation for six days on a home-coming trans-Atlantic liner.

§ 6

The most fiery, eloquent and persuasive plea to patriotism, the most impassioned and hypnotic appeal for youth to serve its country in time of war peril, is not one-half so convincing, not one-half so irresistible, not one-half so influential and so successful as a strikingly becoming uniform.

§ 7

Whenever there is a war, the home-loving Vigilantes of all countries always accuse the Jews of belonging to the enemy nation, whatever it is.

§ 8

The victories of peace endure only until someone invents a new gun.

VII. ATTITUDE TOWARD AMERICA

§ 1

An Outline of the History of the Progress of the United States of America from 1775 to 1925.— George Washington did not have a single decoration from a foreign government. Otto Kahn has twenty-six.

§ 2

It is a peculiarity of the American mind that it regards any excursion into the truth as an adventure in cynicism. Let a writer or any one else clear his eyes and make an effort to get under the pretty blanket which Americans like to throw over ugly facts and to set forth his findings and at once he will be dubbed a carper, a detractor, a shrew. It is not that the American mind does not know better, for it does; it knows that the exploratory person in point is not exactly what it calls him. It is, rather, that the American mind seeks thus, like an ostrich with its head in the sand or a jail-bird who tears off his calendar hind end foremost, to blink the humiliations of truth and to foster the comforts of illusion.

§ 3

If it be un-American to disparage and detract from much that is American, it is, equally, un-Borneoan to disparage and detract from much that is held in patriotic esteem in Borneo.

§ 4

The smart American drinks St. Emilion, Graves, St. Julien and Macon, the beverages of French peasants. He plays mah jong, the game of Chinese coolies. He wears, on Sundays, a cutaway coat, the garb of English clerks. His melodic taste is for jazz, the music of African niggers. He eats alligator pears, the food of Costa Rican billy-goats. . . .

§ 5

A Crescendo Moving Picture of American Generals.—General George Washington was a gay fellow with the girls. General Andrew Jackson was a customer of parlors of physiological joy and swore like a Turk. General Winfield Scott was a boozer. General Ulysses S. Grant was an even bigger one. General Nelson A. Miles was an

excellent poker player.   General John J. Pershing
belongs to the Y. M. C. A.

§ 6

The most certain way in which to impress, persuade and convince the American public about the
virtue of anything, from a war to a pill, is, first,
to devise a catchy slogan and, secondly, to make
sure that it has in it only a minimum of accuracy.
The invention of the catch-phrase, "To Make the
World Safe for Democracy", was a masterpiece
of boob-fetching, and a not less masterful instance
of the technic was that displayed by the late Creel
Press Bureau when it enlisted the services of a
number of experienced writers of popular fiction
to employ their art to make the public swallow
the slogan, and the war, whole.   Castoria is an
excellent cathartic, one of the best there is, but
who ever actually heard a child cry for it?   Yet
the slogan has moved the public quite as effectively as the philtre itself.   The public believes
that children bawl for Castoria and are completely
blue and miserable unless it be given to them.   In
the same way, slogans have persuaded the public
to believe, at least to a degree, that a certain express
train goes as fast as a cannon ball, that one's father
(or dad, as he is affectionately known) smokes

just one brand of tobacco, that all housewives eventually come to use a certain brand of baking flour, that a certain western city's fame was gained entirely from a beer that was brewed there, that Wilson whiskey was the best on the market and that's all there was to it, that life, liberty and the pursuit of happiness are vouchsafed equally to all citizens of the Republic, that a certain circus, which has been practically the same for the last decade, is bigger and better every successive year, that a dog can recognize his master's voice only if it is recorded on a certain phonograph, that if a pocket camera doesn't bear a specific name it isn't a pocket camera, that, before Prohibition, all members of fashionable clubs drank certain ready-made bottled cocktails, and a thousand other such things. The American public thinks in terms of catch-phrases. It remembers the Maine, says it with flowers, and needs no stropping or honing to sharpen its gullibility.

§ 7

In the recent concerted critical attack upon the principles, ethics and conduct of the American journalistic press, it strikes me that the critics, though they state what is undoubtedly true, nevertheless finally negotiate what is true of the jour-

91

nalistic press the world over. The criticism they make of American journalism describes English, French, German and other foreign journalism quite as appositely and trenchantly. If the general standard of American newspaper morals is low, it is no lower than that of the general run of European newspapers, and this applies alike to the owners of those newspapers and to the hired men who make them.

To say that the average American newspaper reporter is a cheap and ignoble fellow is to imply that the average English, French or German reporter is not a cheap and ignoble fellow. The implication is without warrant. For, though it is pretty uniformly agreed that newspaper reporting is a profession that, save in the case of very young men, attracts the riff-raff, the disappointed, the incompetent and the mentally pink in the field of what, by stretching several thousand points, may in this connection be called the world of letters, it is not true that the men it attracts in America are worse, in any respect, than those it attracts in other countries. As a matter of fact, the American reporter—I am, plainly enough, speaking not of the higher grade of reporters but of the lower and middle grades—is much the superior of his foreign colleague. His resource, his independence, his achievements—all are greater than those of the English, French or German newspaper reporter of his class. Not a week passes that American newspaper reporters do not excel the pick of European newspaper reporters. They write better, as a general rule, and they know more about reporting. The European reporter, as all know who have ever come into close professional or even lay contact with him, is not to be compared with the American, however relatively questionable the latter may be. The English reporter is a tidier fellow, and he is generally a better educated man, but as a reporter he is the inferior of the American. Both are always obviously at the mercy of the shadowy "policy" whip at their rear, but, even so, the American is the freer agent. The French reporter is hardly to be called a newspaper reporter in the strict meaning of the word: he is a mere alibi. He pretends to get news in order that his boss may call what he publishes a newspaper. Unless that boss sent reporters out onto the street for the look of the thing, even the French would refuse to regard his product as a newspaper. The German reporter, at least at the present time, combines in himself the worst features of both the English and French reporter.

What holds true of reporters, holds equally true

of the captains of the journalistic industry. The American newspaper owner is surely no worse than the English, French or German. As a matter of record, he is, as a usual thing, a lot better. Aside from a few readily apparent exceptions, he is more honest, more fearless, more resourceful and infinitely more successful. For every American Munsey, there are three European Munseys. The deduction is simple. The generality of American journalism as we have it today is in a disgraceful state for the reason that journalism the world over is, for the major part, in a disgraceful state. Journalism, to a considerable degree, has ceased to be the profession of intelligent, idealistic and charming gentlemen. It has become the profession of public office seekers, title hunters, social pushers, dollar diddlers, mountebanks, and cads.

§ 8

The cornerstone of successful American daily journalism is scandal. The moment politicians stop stealing the public's money, women begin to obey the seventh commandment and men go back to using their fists instead of revolvers, that moment will three-fourths of our newspapers slide down the chute to the poor-house.

§ 9

Those Americans whose ancestors came over on the *Mayflower* are given to a contemptuous looking-down on those Americans whose ancestors came over on somewhat more modern and vastly more comfortable Cunarders.

§ 10

I take a five-cent piece out of my pocket and look at it. It bears the head of an American Indian. Above the Indian is the inscription "Liberty". For the name of every Indian who is permitted the measure of liberty of the white man in the United States, I offer one of the aforementioned five-cent pieces.

§ 11

The European notion that Americans are always in a hurry, that they think always and only of business and never permit themselves the leisure that an European permits himself goes quickly to pieces the moment one considers the evidence. More radio machines and phonographs are sold to the square head in America than in any other country. The daily crowds at baseball games in America are a thousand times larger than the crowds at any sporting spectacles in any other country and the moving picture audiences, the statistics show, are seventeen hundred and thirty times as large. Individually, and more accurately, the American male goes to a ball game four times to every once that an European goes to a relative sporting exhibition, and to a movie six times for every once that his foreign brother goes to a similar exhibition. The Ford pleasure car figures show that eighty Americans use Fords for other than business purposes to every foreigner who uses one for the same purposes. And so it is down the statistical line. The average American lives a more leisurely life than the average European. He is in point of fact, with perhaps the Spaniard as the sole exception, the greatest waster of time in existence.

§ 12

The voice of the Lord God Almighty, Maker of Heaven and Earth, as periodically reflected by the people of the United States and their self-imposed laws and regulations, severally by municipalities and States or collectively by the Union:

1. God is against cigarettes.
2. God is against playing cards.
3. God is against advertisements of whiskey.

4. God is against whiskey.

5. God is against billiards.

6. God is against pool.

7. God is against moving pictures showing a man kissing a woman for longer than ten seconds.

8. God is against *La Vie Parisienne*.

9. God is against the plays of Avery Hopwood.

10. God is against Eugene V. Debs.

11. God is against Little Egypt.

12. God is against playing baseball on Sunday.

13. God is against carrying a pocket flask.

14. God is against dancing after eleven P. M.

15. God is against dancing after twelve P. M.

16. God is against dancing after one A. M.

17. God is against dancing at all.

18. God is against secret societies.

19. God is against German opera.

20. God is against public speaking by a member of the I.W.W.

21. God is against Boccaccio, Balzac, Fielding, Anatole France, D. H. Lawrence and Cabell.

22. God is against bare knees.

23. God is against allowing children to appear on the stage.

24. God is against the female leg.

25. God is against congregating on street corners.

26. God is against letting poor men sleep on the benches in public parks.

27. God is against birth control.

28. God is against speaking in public on birth control.

29. God is against sending birth control literature through the mails.

30. God and the late Hon. Jim Mann are fraternity brothers.

31. God is against the minority at all times.

32. God is against all illiterates save those who are American born.

33. God is against a trade alliance of proficient business men against their inferiors.

34. God believes that a Mississippi Negro bootblack is the equal of John Singer Sargent.

35. God is against one-piece bathing suits.

36. God believes that Sholom Asch's play, "The God of Vengeance," is very immoral stuff and that the actors who play it should be arrested, tried by a jury, convicted of a criminal offense, and either be fined or locked up in the hoosegow.

37. God believes that if the United States didn't look after South America, South America would go to the dogs.

38. God is against Socialists, but loves all Republicans and Democrats.

39. God is against the hula-hula.

40. God is against walking on the grass in public parks.

41. God believes that all bathing beaches should be lighted up with acetylene lamps at night and that policemen should arrest any couple discovered holding hands.

42. God believes that a teamster whose horse is lazy and won't work and who taps the nag emphatically across the rear in order to make him work should be promptly arrested.

43. God is against prize-fighting.

44. God doesn't believe in betting on the races.

45. God is against masked ball merrymakers wearing their masks on the street on the way to the party, and believes that they should be arrested if they do so.

46. God is opposed to American women wearing aigrettes.

47. God is against anyone bringing banana seed into the United States.

48. God believes that the Japanese are inferior to the Armenians.

49. God believes that it is wrong to shoot and kill rabbits in Rhode Island between January 1st and November 1st, but quite jolly to do so from November 1st to January 1st. He also believes that it is wrong to pot deer in New Hampshire from December 16th to the following December 1st, but

99

good sport to do so from the 1st to the 15th. However, He is against persons living in Colorado, Indiana, Iowa and Kansas shooting deer at any time.

50. God believes that lake trout of $14\frac{1}{2}$ inches should be thrown back into the water but that trout ½ an inch longer, as served, for example, at the Ritz, make a very desirable and tasty dish.

51. God believes that it was necessary to pass a law making it moral to sell automobile tires on Sunday in New York State.

52. God is against pink lemonade.

53. God believes that Rodin is a very dirty fellow.

54. God believes that it is wrong for anyone to work in any mercantile or commercial house in Utah after six o'clock, except for the six days preceding His birthday, Christmas, which may be appropriately celebrated by working until midnight.

55. God believes that separate wash-rooms should be supplied for Negro laborers in Missouri.

56. God holds that no chiropodist in Connecticut shall call himself a Doctor, but that it is all right in any other State.

57. God believes that the bed sheets in hotels and lodging houses in Indiana should be of a certain exact size, regulated by law.

58. God is of the belief that if a man shines

shoes or sells flowers on Sunday in Alliance, Ohio, he should be fined, and that if he does it a second time he should be sent to jail for thirty days.

59. God is against the delivery of ice on Sunday in Omaha, Neb.

60. God believes that if a man or woman writes a poem (for paid publication in a magazine) on Sunday in Utah, he or she should be arrested.

61. God believes that it is wrong to drive an automobile on Sunday in Ocean Grove, New Jersey.

62. God believes that music should not be played on Sunday in Berkeley, Cal.

63. God believes that it is all wrong to sell a bottle of ketchup on Sunday in the Bronx.

64. God believes that all persons in Tangier, Va., who do not go to church should be compelled by ordinance to stay indoors during the period of church services and under no circumstances be permitted to go out.

65. God is against buying, selling, or smoking a cigarette in Utah.

66. God believes that no Nebraska girl should be permitted to wear a short skirt.

67. God believes it is wrong to tip a servant in Iowa.

68. God holds it illegal to teach the doctrine of evolution in Texas and Tennessee.

69. God believes that children should not be allowed to attend private schools in Oregon.

70. God says that one must not whistle on Sunday in Massachusetts.

71. God doesn't believe in shaving on Sunday in Arizona.

§ 13

The idea still persists in certain quarters that the larger eastern American universities are educational institutions, that is, places to which young men go in search of knowledge. Curiously enough, the idea is true. But its truth is not quite that which the majority of persons believe it to be. The larger eastern American universities *are* educational institutions and they are, too, places to which young men go in search of knowledge, but the education and knowledge that the average young man gets from them has infinitely less to do with Latin, Greek, epistemology, economics, the Purvamimansa system of Hindu philosophy and the Pali grammar of Kachchayana than with Irving Berlin's latest fox-trot, the right kind of pleated trousers, the way to make drinkable synthetic gin, the technic of what Scott Fitzgerald calls necking, athletic diversions, and the trick of going to New York for a day without the faculty catching on to it. For one boy who is athirst for knowledge,

102

who wishes to learn the difference between the
theory of least squares and anthropogeography
and what distinguishes the Battle of Eckmühl from
the Portuguese navigator Mascarenhas and the
poetry of Swinburne, there are a dozen who care
no more for knowledge of any shape, size or kind
than a burnt-cork salesman cares for Dahomey.
Ask twenty boys at one of these educational cabarets which they would rather know: the history
of French literature or Ann Pennington's telephone
number, and if nineteen do not answer the way I
think they would, I am a very unobservant beagle.

§ 14

The old live romance of America, so infinitely
brilliant and exciting, has been slowly put through
the sausage machine of commercialism and moral
prosaicism and come out a dead thing. The Indian has been converted from a flaming red arrow
of the forests into a dime sideshow exhibit at
Coney Island and a ham in Wild West exhibitions.
The train robber of the plains has become a con-
tributor to the *Saturday Evening Post*, and the
hobo of the railroad ties has been transformed into
an autobiographer and popular magazine poet.
The three-card-monte and shell-game professors of
yesteryear are now oil stock salesmen; the old

103

river-boat gamblers are rich bootleggers and members of respectable society, with ringside tables at the best night clubs and houses at Palm Beach. The American sailor has become a member of the Y. M. C. A. and a follower of Pola Negri, Monte Blue and Norma Talmadge. The cowboy reads the *Adventure* magazine by day and sits in a movie theatre by night. The old romantic swindlers of Wall Street, those giants of venturesomeness and audacity twenty and thirty years ago, have reformed, have bought pews in the swell local churches and have become chairmen of membership committees in golf clubs. The romance of American names, too, is fast passing into the limbo of the forgotten: streets in American cities that once were named after American Indian tribes and American flowers and American trees are now labeled with numerals; American drinks with their peculiarly flavorous American names have been suppressed by Prohibition; hotels, once adorned with names that suggested the old trading posts and forts and frontiers, are now named after European cafés, chateaux and golf links; drinking and eating houses, once emblazoned with names racy of the soil, are now called after Spanish and French bordellos. Wyoming Avenue has become Sixty-first Street; the Manhattan cocktail is no more; the American House has become the Belle-

vue or the Touraine; the Silver Dollar has become
the Club de Seville. . . . Let us draw out our
handkerchiefs and shed a tear.   Gone is the America of our boyhood!

§ 15

Thumbnail Impression of the Composite American Aristocracy after a Perusal of a Leading Society Journal.—Roger Stuyvesant Pingley, whose
marriage to Hildegarde Lucille Potter-Potter will
take place next week, is one of the recognized
leaders of the younger set of old guard society.
He is of Flemish-English extraction, his father,
the late Ebenezer Augustus Pingley, born in New
York in 1836, having descended from a family
from Antwerp, long settled in the Mohawk Val-
ley.   His grandfather, Elijah Pingley, married,
in 1810, Abigail, daughter of Eustace Frawley, of
Middlesex, England.   The mother of Roger Stuyvesant Pingley and of his brother Archibald, husband of Marie Sickle, was Harriet Peters,
daughter of Lucius Dart.   The Dart family traces
origin to Duncan, who fought under William the
Conqueror.   Duncan's oldest son, Henry, was
owner of a country seat at Millersboro, Essex,
while his fourth son, Albert, was owner of a country seat at Fullersboro, Sussex.   The Darts were

established in New England early in the Seventeenth Century, being the first settlers at Martinsville, Vermont. Roger Stuyvesant Pingley is head of the shoe department at Gimbel's.

§ 16

The Americano has at least one reason for getting down on his knees every night and offering up a prayer of thanks to the Almighty, and that is the absence at Washington of a Ministry of Fine Arts such as that maintained by the French government. Imagine a department of this kind as it would be filled and operated in these grand and glorious States! Who would be appointed its head under the current system of selection? The odds are one hundred to one that if Edward W. Bok, Ph.D., LL.D., were not the pick, Augustus Thomas or Adolph Zukor would be. Honors and decorations would promptly be conferred upon Zane Grey, Henry van Dyke, Morris Gest, Augustus Lukeman, Hermann Hagedorn, Charlie Chaplin, the Rev. Dr. John Haynes Holmes, Edgar A. Guest, D. W. Griffith, Isaac Marcosson and Johnny Farrar. A gala annual banquet would be held at the New Willard at which eloquent addresses on art would be made by bankers who had been brought on as suckers for endowment funds. The

National Institute of Arts and Letters would march *en masse* to the ceremonies in cap and gown, and would be headed by Isham Jones' jazz band playing George Gershwin's latest masterpiece. Harry Hansen would get salubriously stewed and bite off William Lyon Phelps' ear, and Phelps, in turn, would spill his *consommé Créole* on the heiress to Amy Lowell's cigar. A toast would be offered to the memory of those two great *litterateurs,* the MM. Woodrow Wilson and Theodore Roosevelt. and Dreiser, Cabell, Red Lewis and the rest of such dismal failures who had been left out in the cold would despairfully foregather in the back room of some Union Hill, N. J., pot-house and see who could hit the spittoon oftenest in sixty-five shots.

§ 17

How much does the poor union working man, abused and oppressed by capital, actually work? Let us see.

There are 365 days in the year. Of these, 52 are Sundays. That leaves 313 days. Of these, 52 are Saturdays or half-work days. Half of 52 is 26. That leaves 287 days. Of these, there are New Year's Day, Lincoln's Birthday, Washington's Birthday, Decoration Day, the Fourth of July, Labor Day, Columbus' Birthday, Thanksgiving Day and Christmas—all holidays, which leaves 278 days. In addition there are such State holidays as Arbor Day, such holidays as St. Patrick's Day and various religious holidays like Good Friday—an average of, let us say—to put it low—a half dozen. That leaves 272 days. The average human being, according to the best medical statistics available, is ill, taking one year with another, at least twelve days each year, and is then unfit for work. That leaves 260 days. The average working man's vacation period amounts to two weeks or, less the two Sundays and two half-Saturdays already counted, eleven days. That leaves 249 days. A day contains 24 hours, eight of which are the union limit of labor. Eight is one-third of 24, hence the working man works for one-third of 249 days. That is 83 days. On each of these 83 days he takes an hour off for lunch. Eighty-three hours amounts approximately to three and one-half days. That leaves 79½ days. Now, it is impossible for any human being to work continuously, without periodic rest, for seven hours. There must be time to stop for breath, to ease up the muscles, to take the crick out of one's back, to wait until one's helper is ready, to light one's pipe, to wipe the sweat from one's forehead—to do any number of such things. In a working period of seven hours, at least one hour is necessarily so wasted. That means, in 79½ days, 79½ hours—or approximately three and one-third days. That leaves approximately 76⅙ days. The average poor union working man thus actually works just 76⅙ days out of the 365. When you have figured out the percentage, breathe a sympathetic sigh for him.

§ 18

Sings Ko-Ko in "The Mikado": ". . . Then the idiot who praises, with enthusiastic tone, all centuries but this, and every country but his own."

I fear that I, for one, have in the past been not wholly free from the good Ko-Ko's disfavor, particularly as regards the second article of his animadversion. I have praised, with enthusiastic tone, English letters, French drama, German beer and music, Hungarian girls, Italian art, Turkish morals, Danish pastry, Swedish bathtowels, Greek sculpture, Spanish wines, Russian ballets, Swiss Alps and cheese, Dutch painting and Cuban cigars, as opposed to the like products of my own native land. I have praised, with not less enthusiastic tone, the British form of government as opposed to that of my own country, the free gayety of the French people as opposed to the blue and restricted gayety of my own people, the tolerance of the church of Italian Rome as opposed to the bigotry of the Methodist domination of the United States, and the integrity of the German nation as opposed to the hypocrisy of my own nation. If all this has set me down as an idiot, an idiot I am. But, whether it be true that I am and have been an idiot or not, it seems to me to be time to shout "Whoa!" to the current sweeping disparagement, on the part of certain sepulchral and misguided citizens, of a Republic that, for all its obvious and transparent defects, has yet perhaps as many things to recommend it as any other country warmed by the sunshine of an all-wise and forgiving Siddhartha.

I resent the suppressed snickers of the butler that greet the United States whenever its name is mentioned at an alien dinner table. I resent the intimation of cultivated foreigners—and cultivated Americans no less—that the United States is a mere ethical and æsthetic outhouse for the obscene use of themselves and others like them. This is hardly the case. The United States may be run by rogues, but so is France, and so is Italy, and so is England. It may be a money-grubbing nation; so is France, and so is Italy, and so is England. It may be worked for all it is worth by profiteers; so is present-day Germany. And it may exalt the stockbroker above the artist and

the automobile manufacturer above the conductor
of a symphony orchestra; so, *as* a nation, does almost every other nation under the heavens. These
are absurd charges. A nation, whatever its name,
and whatever the color of its flag, is at bottom, and
essentially, a mere mob. And a mob is always
cheap, always shoddy, and infinitely ignorant.
One thinks of a country, one's own or someone's
else, not in terms of the millions of soup colora-
turos who compose it, but in terms of its minority
of educated and civilized men. My country has
such men as other countries have them. It has
them perhaps in not such great number, but it is
getting more of them year by year. The old order changeth. The younger generation, so to
speak, is not only knocking at the back door; it is
already in the kitchen, with the cook on its knee.
. . . The sound of artillery is in the air.

But enough of such prophecy, in all probability
wrong. Let the band strike up with the existing
facts. The United States is today, as it has been
for the last fifteen years, the most thoroughly comfortable country to live in that one can find in
the atlas. Its trains, taxicab service, bathrooms,
ventilating systems, street buses, subways, ele-
vated roads, hotels (in the aggregate), street-
cleaning devices, the innumerable small things
that contribute to make daily life easy and endur-

able—these are not matched by any other country. There is not a railroad in all of Europe one-fiftieth so well managed and so well run as the Pennsylvania. There isn't one that serves as respectable food in its dining-cars as the Baltimore and Ohio. There aren't in the world as satisfactory taxicabs as the original American "Yellows". Aside from the Ritz hotels, which are the same wherever one finds them, the United States can match every Adlon with a half dozen Plazas, every Bayerischer-Hof with a half dozen Statlers. The American bathroom—and here recall George Moore's celebrated philosophy—makes every other bathroom look like a country shanty amid the sunflowers. American heating apparatus, American barber-shops, American writing paper, American bootblacking entrepreneurs, American telephone service (in every large city save New York), American elevators, American drugstores, American coins and currency—these, too, lead the world in point of merit and efficiency. One need not emit a cackle at the crass materialness of such an argument. It is only the poseur who pretends that these are not, many of them, of a high importance in the scheme of life of mortal man and in his ever-present quest for tranquility of mind, peace of spirit, and bodily ease. Let the disbeliever try to find a decent pair of garters in Europe when he has broken the pair he brought over with him from America; let him go and have his hair cut; let him hurriedly try to buy a shirt that fits him; let him try his luck at having an aching tooth pulled or filled; let him try to find a comfortable pair of European shoes; let him try to get a satisfactory witch hazel to use after shaving; let him search for a strikable match in France, an ungreasy dish in Italy, a damp cigar in England, a dry bed sheet in Norway, a pen that he can write with in Greece, a mild cigarette in Russia, a hair brush in Spain, a dose of castor oil in Rumania, a decent cup of coffee in Portugal, or the most necessary if unmentionable article of human comfort in Denmark—let him essay this repertoire of likes and needs, or any part of it, and then ask him —if he is one part human—whether he cares to see New York harbor again, and how soon!

But have done with such base things, and to the higher reaches. The general literary taste of the United States at the present time—comparing the list of fiction and non-fiction best sellers with the same lists, where they are available, in Europe—is superior to that of England, France, Germany or Italy. Save alone Berlin, the dramatic taste of New York is at the present time considerably higher than that of any European capital. It is five times superior to that of London, and three times superior to that of Paris. America provides a larger and more lucrative audience for opera, symphony concerts and the recitals of first-rate musicians than any other country. The level of intelligence and artistic perception is much lower in the higher stratum of the American people than in the same stratum of the European, but the mass of one country is not much different, as I have observed, from the mass of another. The American yokel and the German peasant, the American boob and the English boob, the American hick and the French hick are brothers in ignorance under the cuticle. The difference between the obscene show that the United States and that, say, France provides is simply the difference between the show that Ringlings' circus provides on the one hand and that Walter L. Main's provides on the other. It is merely a matter of magnitude. The essentials are common to both.

Our politics are a vulgar shambles? So are the French. Our foreign policy is hypocritical? Look to England's! Our society is a cheap cuckooing of the English? True enough; there a clay pipe breaks to the credit of the score of the opposition. Our art is still in a crude state of development. Again true; but it is making progress. The American short story leads the world; the American etching is rapidly forging to the modern front rank; the American Victor Herbert, but recently laid to rest, is the superior of Lehar or Eysler or Kalmann or Fall; the American novel and drama gain stature and dignity steadily. Dreiser, Cabell, Lewis, Hergesheimer, Cather, O'Neill come on apace. And to return briefly to the shorter form of fiction, there is not a writer in Europe today doing finer work than the American Sherwood Anderson or Ruth Suckow. American criticism, on the higher levels, if inferior to the English and German, is miles ahead of the French and Spanish. American sculpture and painting and music are still either downright bad or in the process of finding themselves. These lie in the lap of time. The France of today is in the hands of self-seeking politicians; the Germany in the hands of profiteers; the England in the hands of clever and unscrupulous business men. If the United States, in turn, is in the hands of knaves and rascals—and what is worse, ignoramuses— where the great difference to a man with his eyes to the stars and with a cellar full of pre-Prohibition Scotch, gin, wine and Cointreau?

§ 19

Among the reasons promiscuously assigned for the falling off in enlistments in the Navy, I notice that what is perhaps as good a reason as any other is conspicuously absent. Although the truth is not a pleasant one, it remains that the sailor boy has come under a cloud and that this stigma is responsible for the disinclination of young men, who would otherwise be glad to enlist, to do so. The cloud that I allude to, obviously enough, is that which reflects upon the gender of the sailor boy's morals, which, incidentally, has grown to such proportions that it is today one of the favorite bases of burlesque show and barroom jests, and which has contrived to cast suspicion upon the class as a whole. That this suspicion is largely unwarranted is, equally obviously, true. For one sailor derelict in the matter of what may be termed 100 per cent American, if not always Anglo-Saxon, sex morals, there are unquestionably a dozen or more who are as gamogenetically upright and praiseworthy as so many guinea pigs. But the good have suffered with the bad, and as a result the sailor boy of the moment is often the target of a cruel humor which he in no wise deserves.

§20

More buncombe is practised in the matter of what is called scientific research than in any other field of human enterprise, saving only antique furniture, Russian caviar and politics. We are thus currently entertained by a plenitude of scalings of inaccessible mountain peaks, expeditions to the North Pole, crossings of the Atlantic in twenty-foot sail-boats, dinosaurus-hunting trips into African jungles, explorations of Egyptian grave-yards, Hindustan butterfly quests and airplane circlings around the Woolworth tower which have little or nothing to do with true science and which result in no more important contributions to the sum of scientific knowledge than movies for the news reels. Most of these expeditions, investigations and experiments are heavily backed by suckers or by oafs with a scientific bee in their belfrys. Last year alone it is estimated that the total outlay for such pseudo-scientific monkeyshines approximated six millions of dollars. Vastly more might be done for science if the suckers and posturers would put their money in savings banks and keep out only enough to buy Alexis Carrel a couple of boxes of good cigars.

§ 21

A study of American humor should not fail to include a treatise on the trademarks that American

merchants select for their goods. Many of these
trademarks possess an intrinsic jocosity beside the
richness of which the best Ford or monkey gland
joke must hang its head in shame. The processes
of reasoning whereby the merchants in question
have arrived at them as apt and suitable emblem-
atica for their wares is difficult to make out, as
they often are no more accurately descriptive of the
said wares than so many bootleggers' labels. A
well-known cathartic water is thus called Pluto,
after a Greek mythological god chiefly famous for
his rape of a sweet chuck hight Proserpine, while
another cathartic is named after the Roman mythological figure, Castor, who was chiefly famous for
his dexterity in handling horses. Again, a certain
brand of tooth-picks bears the name of Edward
VII, who once kicked a man off the terrace at Monte
Carlo for offending his vision with a molar-poker.
Still again, a beer has been dubbed Phoenix,
which beer, if one were to accept the Oriental
mythological term, would promptly confer im-
mortality upon its imbiber. Still further, a well-
known skin cream bears the trademark, Pompeiian,
its christener being doubtless unaware that Pompeii
was ruined by eruptions. A hundred such trademarks may be readily called to mind. I expect
any day to hear of an American manufacturer who
puts out a rat-trap called "Liberty".

§ 22

In a review of a recently published novel, I find the phrase, "the artificial window-box life of New York". It is a phrase that, in one form or another, one constantly encounters in the writings of men who live in the hinterland or of others who, imported to New York, long still in their hearts for the great open cow-pastures. What is in the phrase? So far as I can make out, after prolonged conferences with myself, absolutely nothing.

The notion that life in New York is in the aggregate any more artificial than life in a small town is the not uncharacteristic reasoning of such persons as have been born to believe that human nature is forthright and honest in a farmhouse but is quickly perverted and corrupted if it takes a suite at the Ritz. That there is an artificial side to life in the metropolis, no one disputes. But this phase of life is confined very largely to more or less temporary visitors who are no more really New Yorkers than real New Yorkers are Parisians when they cut up in the Paris cafés and peepshows. The New Yorker, by and large, leads a life that is no more artificial, when you come to look at it closely, than the life led by the average country-town lout. What is more, even the good-time-Charlie New Yorker, the flashier type of New

Yorker, isn't at bottom much different from his country-jake cousin. He dresses better and he spends more money (because he makes more), but in other ways Julius O'Grady and this lady's Colonel—jake and sophisticate—are birds of a feather. Both, to get to the main point at once, are ignoramuses. They have little education, little taste, little distinction—and not the slightest perception of refinement or beauty. Both are dolts. But their lives are cast upon much the same intrinsic plan, however varying the details. The rube lives in a frame house with the *châlet de nécessité* a block away; the New Yorker lives in an apartment with the *cabinet d'eaux* three feet from his bed. The New Yorker drinks genuine Holloway gin; the rube, home-made apple-jack. The New Yorker dances jazz to Paul Whiteman's jazz band; the rube dances the polka and the Virginia reel to the grocery boy's fiddle. The New Yorker negotiates his rendezvous on the Albany night boats or in Atlantic City; the rube negotiates his in his phaeton or in a hayloft, and he negotiates them oftener, if the statistics do not deceive us, than the city man. The New Yorker, when he tires of his wife and can't stand her any longer, kicks her out and divorces her; the rube, when he tires of his and can't stand her any longer, goes on living

120

with her and making the rest of his own and her life miserable.

And so it goes. If life in New York is artificial, life in Newtsville and Sauk Centre is equally so. If the New Yorker pivots his life on the making of money, what about the farmer? If the New Yorker, in the pursuit of money, cheats and swindles, what about the farmer? If the New Yorker does not go to church on Sunday, how much does the rube consider God on Monday, Tuesday, Wednesday, Thursday, Friday and Saturday? If the New York flapper bobs her hair, rolls her stockings, smokes cigarettes and is indiscreet, so to speak, in taxicabs, what about the country girl when the lights in the front parlor have been turned down and pa has swallowed his chewing tobacco and gone to bed? If the New Yorker sits up at night listening to a cabaret hussy sing "Who Makes the Dressmaker's Daughter When the Dressmaker's Making a Dress?", what about the rube's sitting up at night to listen to the same flapdoodle over the radio? If the New Yorker thinks artificially, the rube doesn't think at all. When I read references to the artificiality of life in New York, indeed, I am reminded of the French peasant who walked two hundred miles to see Paris, who arrived at six o'clock in the morning, who saw a policeman pa-

121

troling his beat in the chilly dawn and who, shaking his head sadly, observed, "Yes, yes, they are true.   Alas, they are true, these stories of the dissipations and artificial life of Paris!   What will happen to our army if its generals stay up all night and raise hell like that one there and don't go home until this time in the morning?"

VIII. ATTITUDE TOWARD ART AND LETTERS

§ 1

All art is hedonistic.

§ 2

The true artist has no goal, but a dozen goals: each a mile-stone on a road whose end is ever some miles beyond the grave into which he is finally laid. It is only the superficial artist who has a goal, and who often achieves it.

§ 3

Fine art, they say, is universal in its appeal. Maybe so. But I should like to observe a Chinese audience listening to Brahms' variations and fugue on a theme by Händel, or a Serb youth reading "Huckleberry Finn", or a Turkish audience viewing Porto-Riche's "Amoureuse", or a gang of lumberjacks in the frozen Northwest around the Venus di Milo.

123

§ 4

Actual experience is often the foe and vanquisher of imagination. What soldier has written of battle as Stephen Crane wrote? What Negro or other Southerner has composed a song of the Southland like Stephen Foster's? What god has ever fashioned an angel as beautiful as one of Raphael's?

§ 5

Beauty is formless. Art is form applied to beauty.

§ 6

The doctrine that sincerity is the first desideratum in a writer, I find difficult to swallow. To ask a writer invariably to believe in everything he writes is to ask a prize-fighter to believe that his opponent is a menace to society, an actor to believe that he *is* Agamemnon, or a patent medicine vendor to believe that he is a saviour of mankind. It is no more necessary that a writer believe what he writes in order to produce first-rate literature than it is necessary for a circus impresario to believe the doctrines of Nero in order to produce a first-rate chariot race.

§ 7

That character is always more important than plot in literature and drama is proved by the fact that we usually remember character in proportion as we forget plot. One remembers Huckleberry Finn; but what was the plot of "Huckleberry Finn"? One remembers Uncle Tom; but what was the plot of "Uncle Tom's Cabin"? One remembers Ben Hur; but what was the plot of "Ben Hur"? And so, too, with Nicholas Nickleby, David Copperfield, Tess of the D'Urbervilles, King Lear, Tom Jones, Fanny Hill, Madame Bovary, Thérèse Raquin, Lord Jim, and a hundred others. The general trends of these one may recall, but the plots have vanished from memory. Only the characters remain.

§ 8

The easiest thing in the world is to attract attention to one's self. All that one has to do to do so, as has often been said, is to walk down the street without one's trousers on. This is the technic embraced by certain of our young adventurers in the field of the arts. These young gentlemen, whose trousers, metaphorically speaking, are not of a sort to attract attention on their own account,

125

take the simplest means out of the difficulty by getting rid of them alogether. The æsthetic boulevard hence currently presents the spectacle of countless young men parading ostentatiously back and forth in their underdrawers and with their *Hemdschweife* hanging out.

The usual manner of thus walking down the thoroughfare takes the shape of a new "form". Unlike their accomplished elders who have been content to attract attention to themselves merely by good work in the more or less time-honored artistic forms, these young men stalk sensational attention with bad work in what may be termed hoochie-coochie forms. This frantic struggle for new forms is the most amusing of Twentieth Century artistic phenomena. Engaged in for the major part by the young—and often lazy—of the æsthetic species, it has resulted in a welter of eye-catching but often intrinsically nonsensical methods and manners of expression which are generally found to contain nothing worth expression. The young gentlemen proceed contrary to the usual custom. Instead of permitting the form to be the natural outgrowth of the subject matter of their imaginations, they arbitrarily invent the form first and then laboriously endeavor to make their ideas fit into it. We thus get an endless series of paintings that are meant to suggest nudes descending stair-

cases in terms of fully clothed geometrical professors ascending staircases, cavatinas written for
harps and xylophones, poems in which the first
line rhymes with the three hundred and fiftieth
and in which each line contains but a single syl-
lable, and plays in which the third act begins in
the middle of the first act and in which the entire
action passes in the rear aisle of the balcony. Out
of this wild orgy have come now and then symp-
toms of something meritorious and permanently
worth-while, but in the mass not much has filtered
through that has been valid.

§ 9

I have, in my editorial capacity, been reading
fiction manuscripts now for exactly eleven years
and four months. In that period, I have read
perhaps 30,000. Meditating these 30,000, I am
brought to the conclusion that I have never yet
found a good one that began in any one of the following ways: 1. "It was in the year so-and-so";
2. "Now, dear reader"; 3. "Long ago, before this
story begins"; 4. "This is the true story of";
5. "Out beyond the line where the sea touched the
sky"; 6. with the description of gathering clouds;
7. with a quotation from Horace; or 8. with the
word "imagine".

§ 10

Is there a college or university in America whose professors of English composition would have given a mark higher than minus one to George Ade, Helen Green, Ring Lardner, Kin Hubbard, Edgar Lee Masters and Walter Hasenclever had they come before them as young, unknown men or women?

§ 11

Not a week passes that I do not get at least three or four invitations to lecture. The requests come in from colleges, women's clubs, little theatres, literary groups, stage societies, chambers of commerce and what not. Do these good people actually wish to hear me lecture? I doubt it. They know my ideas, pro and con, from my writings; if they did not know them, they obviously would not think of inviting me to speak to them. What they want is not to hear what I have to say, but to take a look at me. They are less interested in what I would speak on—since, as I have said, they know it pretty well already—than in what I look like, what kind of clothes I wear, what my voice sounds like, and whether I'll show up drunk or sober. A lecturer is never invited so much as a lecturer as a spectacle. I know that I am not much

128

in the way of a spectacle, so I have the good sense to send back all lecture invitations with a rejection slip.

§ 12

One can generally tell an Irish author without looking at the name attached to the work. The typical Irish vagueness betrays the nationality of the artist. This Irish vagueness—in many cases it is described as mysticism—is not so often the appealing merit that some find it to be as an irritating fault. It is merely the result of a befuddlement of mind which produces either fine poets like Synge or bad dramatists like James Joyce.

§ 13

Leading members of the National Institute of Arts and Letters, together with a record of certain of their most conspicuous achievements, culled from "Who's Who in America":

Aldrich, Richard. Translator of Lilli Lehmann's "How to Sing".

Baker, Ray Stannard. Author of "The Boys' Book of Inventions".

Bishop, William Henry. Author of "Fish and Men in the Maine Islands".

Burton, Richard. Author of "Dumb in June"

(poems), and member of the Simplified Spelling Board.

Chambers, Robert W. Author of "The Common Law", "Police! ! !", "The Restless Sex".

Connolly, James B. Author of "Sonnie Boy's People" and "The U-Boat Hunters".

Crothers, Samuel McChord. Author of "Miss Muffet's Christmas Party".

De Kay, Charles. Author of "Wonders of the Alphabet" for *St. Nicholas Magazine.*

Edwards, Harry Stilwell. Postmaster at Macon, Georgia.

Fernald, Chester B. Adaptor of the play, "Three for Diana".

Firkins, Oscar N. Dramatic critic Minneapolis *Weekly Review.*

Fletcher, Jefferson Butler. 1st Lieut., A. E. F. Author of "The Overture, and Other Poems".

Ford, Worthington C. Author of "The Standard Silver Dollar".

Hagedorn, Hermann. Member of the Loyal Order of Moose.

Hamilton, Clayton. Lecturer at the Finch School for Girls and Miss Spence's School for Girls; continuity writer for the Goldwyn Moving Picture Company.

Hardy, Arthur Sherburne. Author of "Life and Letters of Joseph H. Neesima".

Herford, Oliver. Author of "Cupid's Fair Weather Book", "Jingle Jungles" and "Kitten's Garden of Verses".

Lloyd, Nelson. In newspaper work on New York *Evening Sun;* author of "The Robberies Company, Ltd".

Payne, Will. Author of "When Love Speaks".

Tooker, L. Frank. Author of two novels: "Under Rocking Skies" (1902) and "The Call of the Sea" (1905).

Townsend, Edward W. Author of "Chimmie Fadden".

Whiting, Charles Goodrich. Author of "Ode on the Dedication of the Soldiers' Monument in Springfield, Mass.", "Poem on the 275th Anniversary of the Founding of Springfield", and "Ode on the Musical Opening of the Springfield Auditorium".

Williams, Francis Howard. Author of "At the Rise of the Curtain" (blank verse play).

Thus far not elected to membership, and presumably blackballed: James Branch Cabell, Theodore Dreiser, Sherwood Anderson, Sinclair Lewis, and Carl Sandburg.

§ 14

I sit here, my copious notes on the subject carefully assembled lying close to hand, and prepare to begin an article on the critical idiosyncrasies of the estimable Merejowski. The subject interests me; I am eager to unload my views on it. Yet what keeps my pen from its self-invited job? In the first place, my right ear itches and I stop to scratch it. Then, for some occult and unintelligible reason, my thoughts wander to a band concert I heard several years ago in Madrid, the aforesaid meditation being interrupted in turn by the consciousness that my left shoe is laced too tightly and hurts. In rapid succession, there then pass through my mind—for what reason, God knows!—the thought of how nice it would be to be on a steamer bound for the Caribbean, the memory of a shimmy dancer I once saw in Wilmington, Delaware, the fact that I forgot to call up my bootlegger this morning and replenish my fast disappearing stock of Italian vermouth, certain passages in Graf von Keyserling's "Travel Diary of a Philosopher", the brindisi in "Giroflé-Giroflá", and the feeling that it is high time I had my hair cut. I dip my pen in the ink again, shoot back a cuff and prepare myself anew. Something—doubtless an eyelash—has got into my eye. And my cuff has slid down again. An organ-grinder in the street below has started up a catchy melody: I listen to it for a while. For some inscrutable reason I find my thoughts wandering to Duke's

Hotel, in St. James's Place, London. I notice that I have a little pain in the third finger of my right hand. My specs then need cleaning. Through my head there runs the phrase, *"Ad astra per aspera"*, the motto, I believe, of the State of Nevada. It keeps repeating itself. Now it is my other ear that tickles. I find that I have got ink on my forefinger. I wonder if John D. Rockefeller's wig gets moist and sticky when he plays golf. I light a panatela, burning my finger with the match. I find myself thinking what a funny looking fellow Senator Smoot is. . . .

§ 15

"As you look out of Shaw's window—or rather windows, for the one side of the room is all windows—you see on the left St. Paul's and . . . at your feet the slow-moving Thames sparsely dotted with floating craft, and the prim coat of verdure of the Victoria Embankment, in striking contrast with the Needle of Cleopatra, Eastern in its suggestiveness and mystery. In the middle distance may be discerned the glittering lines of the Crystal Palace, and on clear days one may catch a glimpse of the faraway hills of Kent and Surrey." Thus Archibald Henderson. Never, until I became privy to this news, have I so greatly appreciated the emi-

133

nent Bernard's true calibre. No man not a natural-born genius could write as he has written with such windows in his work-room. The man who could resist looking out of such windows long enough to compose even one-hundredth the amount of work that Shaw has delivered himself of is surely blessed with an artistic urge of uncommonly hefty horse-power.

§ 16

That art is an escape from reality is a contention full of holes. Art is often an escape from fancy and an induction *into* reality. A hundred examples are ready to hand. The drama of Ibsen, Strindberg, Hauptmann and Shaw, the engravings of Hogarth, the novels of Fielding, Zola and Huysmans, the sculpture of Rodin, the paintings of a score of artists from Pollajuolo to Cézanne, the music of Richard Strauss—through art such as this we escape from our dreams into the world of actuality.

§ 17

A book I should like to read—and doubtless there are thousands of ex-youngsters of the 1880's and early 90's who have the same feeling about it as I have—would be a biography, or better still an autobiography, if he is still living, of the man known as Burt Standish, author of the famous Frank Merriwell *literatur*. Who was this Standish; whence came he; what was his history? For week after week and year after year, he poured forth in gaudy-covered brochures the trials and conquests, the adventures and amours, the deeds of derring-do and hair's-breadth escapes of the eminent and well-remembered François, hero and idol of perhaps half the kids of the Republic in the years when Cleveland, Harrison and McKinley held the throne. I doubt, in all seriousness, if there was an American writer of twenty-five and thirty years ago who was so widely known and so widely read by the boys of the time. His readers numbered millions, and included all sorts of young men, rich and poor. For one who read Twain's "Huckleberry Finn" or "Tom Sawyer", there were ten thousand who read Standish's "Frank Merriwell's Dilemma, or the Rescue of Inez" and "Frank Merriwell at Yale, or the Winning Last Quarter-Mile". For one who read Thomas Nelson Page's "Small Boys in Big Boots" or Judge Shute or Archibald Clavering Gunter—or even, for that matter, Horatio Alger, Oliver Optic, or Edward S. Ellis—there were five hundred who weekly followed with avidity the exploits of Standish's magnificent Franz. The little candy and cigar stores of that day, the chief distributing centres of the Standish *opera*, had longer lines of small boys with nickels in their hands every Friday than Barnum's or Forepaugh's circus could ever boast.

The exact number of Standish's works on the illustrious Merriwell, I don't know; but my guess is that it ran well over 15,000. Merriwell was one of the most profitable publishing ventures, I am told, that the country has ever known, and Street and Smith, his impresarios, made a fortune out of him. Standish, unlike many of the other so-called dime novel writers of his era, was a highly moral fellow; he never wrote a suggestive line; his tales always pointed a Sunday School moral; and hence the papas and mamas of the Republic did not curtail his sales by threatening their little Emil with a good licking if they ever caught him reading "such stuff" again. So, as Diamond Dick and Frank Reade and Nick Carter and Old Cap Collier lost in favor with the comptrollers of the family treasury, the favor of Standish and his Merriwell grew and the coins flowed into the former's pocket from hundreds of thousands of boys from the Atlantic to the Pacific. Surely, such a fellow is just as deserving of a biography as the department store owners, safety-razor manufacturers and ham actors whose lives currently line the library shelves.

His influence on American young men was vastly greater than any of these, and the man himself, together with his story, is surely of considerably more interest. Standish was one of America's most peculiarly eminent practitioners of the art of fiction. His curious song deserves to be sung.

§ 18

Hearing that the moving pictures had made enormous strides forward in the last year, I drugged my senses with a quart of synthetic *eau de vie de Danzig* the other evening and betook myself to a large and gaudy cinema-sink to view the wonders and glories of the new artistic dispensation. The bloom was one of that great film favorite's, the M. Zane Grey's; its title, "The Rainbow Trail". The first caption flashed on the screen was as follows:

> For Twelve Long, Weary Years
> Sherrard Had Traveled the
> Desert Looking for His Uncle

Two minutes later found me around the corner again looking at a good old-fashioned artistic dog-fight.

137

§ 19

To speak of morals in art is to speak of a clergyman in a bawdy-house. This is perhaps why the
argument for morals in art is considered by its
numerous sponsors to be so credible.

§ 20

After a genius has taken a theme and made it his
serious own, there is no room left in it for a lesser
man to move about seriously in. All that such a
lesser man can hope to do is to play with the theme
somewhat frivolously, since frivolity is often the
successful refuge of talents that are incapable of
the higher flights.

§ 21

Many literary gents have, I venture, at one time
or another in their lives fashioned for their own
private amusement and the private delectation of
their friends certain confections which, because of
their nature, have never been permitted to see print.
In many instances these esoteric products represent
the best work the gents in question have done; some
of them that have come to my attention, indeed, are
indubitably possessed of a high and genuine quality. Inquiry among writers develops the news, in

point of fact, that it is a rare fellow who hasn't somewhere in his archives a poem, a sketch, an essay, a story or a little play that is close to his heart but that must remain forever hidden from the light because of the birch currently wielded by the professional dung-diggers. Inasmuch, as I have said, a considerable number of these compositions are genuine literature, something should be done about collecting them. Some years ago Mencken and I thought of offering ourselves to the job and of publishing such a collection privately to give to our friends at Christmas-time. But for one reason or another we never went through with it, and the task is therefore still open to other hands.

When we looked over the material for the contemplated volume, we found that there was a wealth of excellent material from which to choose. I can't recollect all of it, but I remember that among the items that we believed should, by virtue of their uncommon quality, be included in the golden treasury were a remarkably amusing playlet in the Maeterlinckian manner by Frederick Arnold Kummer; a gorgeous essay by a New Orleans Maupassant, by name Moïse, called "The Literary Approach"; a rib-busting ironic farce by Randolph Bartlett entitled "Three Like Papa"; a short Oriental sketch by Orrick Johns; a beautifully written and immensely effective story of a certain species of operation by the late Harris Merton Lyon; a long poem, "Oxilene", published privately by the Chamber of Commerce of an Oklahoma city; Edward Ellis' burlesque of the Grand Guignol piece called "The Sacrifice"; an anonymous document entitled "A Royal Fragment"; a short story by Edgar Lee Masters; and a monologue by a layman named Alexander Macdannald on the trials and tribulations of a Virginia rustic. There were twenty or thirty other pieces but, though I recall what they were about, I just now can't recall either their names or the names of their authors. An ideal frontispiece to such a book would be the late George Bellows' magnificent drawing, "Men's Day at the Turkish Bath". I herewith dedicate the job to whoever wants to undertake it.

§ 22

The exponent of that one of the graphic arts which has to do with the laying of paint beautifully upon canvas finds his lot increasingly discouraging in the present-day Republic. In the last fifteen years, his patrons have been recruited less and less from Americans of sound taste and appreciation and more and more from newly-rich American bounders who have made fortunes out of khaki cloth, oil manipulations, bootlegging, gasoline-barrows, chewing gum and enterprises of a piece. It is this latter class of Americans, the most of them with no more actual knowledge of painting than a Hottentot, who currently satisfy their vainglory and posture a fictional culture by unbelting themselves for his works. The old order of American, who had at least a measure of sympathy for and understanding of the artist's aspirations and achievements, has grown poorer as the new order has grown richer, and it can no longer afford the luxuries it once could. And it is thus that the artist is compelled presently to rely for a livelihood not upon persons who can comprehend him and, comprehending, encourage him with their taste, their intelligence and their honestly founded enthusiasm, but upon persons who are not likely to buy one of his paintings until after it has been given the imprimatur of the Sunday rotogravure sections and been reproduced alongside the photographs of Cal Coolidge shaking hands with the Dolly Sisters, Babe Ruth's pet dog, and a scene from Gloria Swanson's latest movie.

It isn't that the artist has to go hungry and sleep on the floor of a Macdougal Alley garret; as a matter of fact, he makes a great deal more money today than he ever made before. It is, rather, that he steadily gets less and less encouragement, both from without and within, to do fine work and more and more, both from without and within, to do merely the hollow and flashy work that the purchasing pack of ex-cloak and suit merchants, ex-army raincoat manufacturers and ex-delicatessen dealers can handily understand. He searches his æsthetic soul, and throws up his hands in despair. The sincerest artist in the world must inevitably lose his sincerity if he is condemned to paint the walls of pig-stys. The sincerest artist in the world must inevitably give up his dreams in disgust when he sees the labors upon which he has expended all his heart-ache and all his joy and all his love hung upon the walls of golf clubs and meat packers' and knit-tie manufacturers' houses. Art can thrive under the patronage of a Lorenzo or a Sixtus IV, but it cannot thrive, though millions be laid at its feet, under the patronage of stock-jobbers, Florida realtors and pants makers.

IX. ATTITUDE TOWARD ALCOHOL

§ 1

In the words of a friend of mine, I drink to make other people interesting.

§ 2

Of the infinite and various philtres devised out of the imagination and ingenuity of the world for the decoration and enchantment of the inside of mortal man, the cocktail, it seems to me, is the most estimable. It has a humor that no other drink has, and it has, in addition, a charm—aye, and romance—that are considerably absent from vessels of other and alien content. The very schedule of its drinking suggests its intrinsic grace. Unlike other bibbables that are guzzled either during or after one's moments of pleasure and joy, the cocktail is ever drunk before: a promise and harbinger of happiness to come. It is the aristocrat of tipples. It does not associate with fish, like sherry, or with cow meat like claret, or with cheese, like Tokay. It is the drink of friends; one seldom, if ever, engages it with a stranger. It is a drink that is reserved for those we like and those who like us. There is no record of a quarrel or fight that has followed its absorption. Such things are reserved for whiskey and the lower elixirs. It has breeding. Unlike champagne, it cares whom it associates with. It is quiet, unostentatious; it avoids flashy places; it is the only drink in the world whose birth is accompanied by tinkling music. Champagne comes into our presence with a loud and vulgar report; whiskey with a common gurgle; the cocktail with a sweet and cool and silvery rattle, as of Eskimo babies at play. It is only when these other potions abandon their genealogical pretensions and engage in miscegenation that they share the cocktail's glory.

The cocktail, once averred George Ade, follows the American flag. That was twenty years ago. The flags of all nations today follow the cocktail. Its fame has spread over the globe, and justly. It has captured the English and the French, the Danes and the Italians. Five o'clock in Piccadilly brings its gin and vermouth and dash of bitters as five o'clock along the grand boulevards brings its iced brandy and gum syrup and dash of Byrrh. It is the gift of smiling America to lackadaisical Europe. It is the international alcoholic Esperanto.

What, strictly speaking, constitutes the charm of

the cocktail? Above everything else, its brevity. It is swallowed at once and *in toto*. Here-it-is-there-it-was! The idiotic hocus-pocus of seidel bumping and of highball sipping is missing entirely. It has the swiftness of a foil's lunge, the directness and point of a witty retort. It is of the very essence of pleasure: it is beautiful and it doesn't last. It claims its all and gives its all in one lovely, fleeting moment. Consider, too, its manner of delivery. The cocktail glass—one should say glasses, so diversified are the kinds that the true connoisseur employs—is perhaps of all drinking vases the most caressing to the eye. Its very shape is appetizing, for in it are lacking the top-heavy rotundity of the champagne glass, the squat dumpiness of the whiskey glass, the stark cylindrical quality of the julep and rickey and highball jardinières and the effeminacy of the sherry and port glasses. The cocktail glass is in aspect for all the world like the opening measures of a Strauss waltz; it is of insinuation, rhythm and melodic promise all compact.

There are, as I have implied, sixty-three different varieties of cocktail glasses that the genuine cocktail professor uses as residences for his divers brews, of which latter, in turn, there are one hundred and eighty-four different and equally delicious species. Roughly speaking, there are therefore only three kinds of cocktails that may be served in a single kind of glass without grievously offending the cognoscenti. To serve a Florestan cocktail, for example, in a Peloponnesus cocktail's glass is, in the eye and palate of the cocktail Corinthian, akin to serving Pilsner in a punch glass. And to see in this discrimination only an affectation is to set one's self down at the outset as one who knows nothing at all about cocktail æsthetics. One would not think of serving champagne in a Burgundy glass or Burgundy in a champagne glass, though both are wines. Similarly, one should not think of serving Daiquiri cocktails in a Martini cocktail glass or Martini cocktails in a Daiquiri cocktail glass, though both are cocktails. It is the same, obviously, with the other cocktails; every third kind calls for its special container. I personally have collected cocktail glasses for the last twenty-five years, my collection at the present time numbering no less than three thousand and eighteen different sets. With these various glasses I have conducted experiments which prove beyond the peradventure of a doubt that the disesteem in which the cocktail is held in certain bourgeois quarters is due in no small degree to the manner of its serving. Indiscriminately to serve different kinds of cocktails in one kind of glass is to offend and disgust the drinker as certainly as if the various dinner-table wines were all to be served to him in one kind of glass. Thus, when you hear a person say that cocktails do not agree with him, it generally means that it is the glass the cocktails have been served in that does not agree with him. The noblest stomach would in time rebel against Rhine wine served in a beer mug or Chartreuse served in a sherry glass. A Bachelor of Cocktails himself similarly cannot long go Twelve Apostles cocktails in a Cleopatra's Ear cocktail glass. Both glasses may be exactly of a size—as, in truth, they are; it is not the size that matters. What matters is the thickness or thinness and the contour of the glass. Imagine drinking Würzburger out of a thin cut-glass tumbler. Imagine drinking Charles Heidsieck 1914 out of a pewter mug. Imagine drinking a Montezuma cocktail out of a Tolstoi's Nipple cocktail glass! The thought staggers one.

The most charming hour of the day, I take it we all agree, is the twilight hour, and the twilight hour is the hour for that most charming of all toddies, the cocktail. What other beverage, indeed, conceivably fits the hour? The day is fading; the evening is dawning. Work is done, and relaxation looms ahead. The factory whistles are losing themselves in the strumming of guitars. A different mood is hovering over the earth, and about to alight. The cocktail baptizes the evening. And

147

the evening slides down the runway, smoothly, gracefully, into the rippling sea of music and laughter and banter and love and heart's ease.

It is the soundest philosophy of alcoholic conduct to drink only with men who have been interesting and women who may be. The waster is not he who wastes his time drinking but he, rather, who wastes his drinking. We owe it to the cocktail to keep it safe from democracy.

§ 3

The emotional effects of alcoholic liquor upon the human nerve centres and psyche are generally, it seems to me, misjudged and misstated. For example, it is maintained that the drinking of alcoholic beverages induces in the drinker a pervading spirit of democracy—that love of one's fellow man and a genial desire to embrace him with both arms and hail him as brother are the distinguishing phenomena of alcoholic indulgence. This is surely not the case. For one man upon whom alcohol exercises this effect, there are fifty in whom drinking inculcates not a democratic, but an aloof and aristocratic, mood. The general effect of alcohol, indeed, is to invest the indulger with a superior air, to make him feel stronger, wiser and more important than he felt before and than he actually is, to create in him a sense of vast *brio* and personal grandeur. This accounts for the frequency of arguments and fights on the part of the partaker. If he were made to feel democratic by alcohol, there would be no such arguments and fisticuffs. Made rather to feel the monarch of all he surveys, he resents the intrusions of lowlier and more sober men, and quickly shows that resentment. Geniality and democracy may lie at the bottom of the first, and sometimes the second, glass, but in the bottom of every glass beyond lies the mood aristocratic.

Another fallacy has to do with the effect of liquor upon women. It is maintained, particularly by fearful old maid school-teachers in the corn, alfalfa and *New Republic* belts, that a partaking of schnapps weakens a woman's morals and places her in a condition where she is unable, mentally and physically, to resist the advances of the predatory male. If this be true, no predatory male has ever noticed it. Instead of weakening a woman's moral defenses, alcohol strengthens them. Alcohol lowers a man's morals and raises a woman's. It places her doubly on guard, intensifies her alertness, takes from the man and gives over to her the reins of leadership and superiority in

149

the personal equation. Whenever you see a Lothario with a black eye, it is a pretty safe assumption that he has got it from some mildly stewed but decidedly wide-awake damsel.

§ 4

Prohibition is legislative birth control applied to rabbits.

§ 5

One encounters them in all corners of Europe, men forlorn of hope, the lines of sorrow upon their faces, the marks of grief and disappointment in their hearts. There is an ache, a longing, in them, and their voices are no longer gay. They are far from home, in happier lands that yet are alien and so are, to them, sad. One I found at Skindle's in Maidenhead, England, a fine fellow whose heart beat bitterly under his striped silk shirt. Another I encountered in a little inn in Vlissingen on the Holland coast, with tears in his fine Celtic blue eyes. Still another, erst a jolly soul, was grumbling in the Rue de Rivoli in Paris, and another still in a large café in Dresden. I found them, these melancholy and transplanted exiles, in Milan, in Buda-Pest, in Lucerne, in Brussels, in far off Athens, working, but heavy-hearted and morose

and wounded behind their forced smiles. They
are the last remains of the great and noble White
Company, soldiers and gentlemen all, the bartenders of the good old days in America.

X. ATTITUDE TOWARD CRITICISM

§ 1

It is a common arraignment of me that I am given to pose and affectation. I have periodically been charged with being an attitudinizer ever since I began writing criticism twenty years ago. Yet the accusation has always puzzled me. In what way am I a poser? I wish that my affable prosecutors would elaborate their indictment somewhat and specify more exactly. Despite this disinclination on their part to elaborate, however, I privilege myself the boon of a few guesses.

I am doubtless considered to be a poser because what I honestly believe and quite as honestly set down in print would obviously and truthfully be a pose on the part of my critics were they to pretend to believe it and duly set it forth. What I mean by this is simply that these estimable gentlemen accuse me of having ideas which, being contrary to the ideas on the same subjects that they themselves have, seem to them to be merely the result of a desire on my part to give a show at their

expense to the profit of my own vainglory. This
is the usual attitude of persons with whose ideas
and prejudices one's own ideas and prejudices happen to be in more or less violent discordance, and
it is quite understandable. It is therefore entirely
natural that when, for example, I, who have been
reviewing plays steadily for two decades, say that
I presently get more pleasure out of a Guitry farce-
comedy than out of an Ibsen play, I should be regarded as a poser by a younger man who, having
been at reviewing for only a few years, still finds
the play of the Norwegian Henri vastly new and
engaging. And it is no less natural that when I,
whose American blood has in it thick and poison-
ous strains of European, by that great calamity am
constitutionally brought to view the world somewhat differently from the way in which a $99^{44}/_{100}$
per cent American views it, I should be narrowly
scrutinized by the latter as being of a suspicious
integrity.

I am often reproached with being a professional
dissenter, with trying frequently to gain an audience for myself by posturing a belief which is in
direct opposition to the belief held at the moment
by the majority. If the frequent holding of beliefs which are in direct opposition to the beliefs
held at the moment by the majority constitutes professional dissent, then, true enough, I am such a

dissenter. For the general run of criticism in America often seems to me to be completely fly-blown and idiotic, and I take pleasure in saying so in terms that are impolite and unmistakable. What is more, I have off and on taken pleasure in saying so for many years, and if le Papa Bon Dieu pleases, shall take pleasure in saying so for many more years to come. I have not, however, said so, as I have been accused of doing, merely to gather a crowd in front of my tent. As a matter of fact, the crowd in front of my tent has never been a large one. It has been made up almost entirely of the minority of persons who, like myself, happen to disagree with the majority. While it is true that I have often written for newspapers (for seven years I wrote for a syndicate of forty-two leading American journals) and also for magazines of a tremendous circulation, I have never for a moment flattered myself that more than one-fiftieth of my readers in such publications agreed with me, or that more than one-hundredth understood accurately what I was driving at.

I am, of course, like almost any man who has been at the writing desk as long as I have, able to give a sufficiently good show to interest the doodles even when they are not sufficiently intelligent to understand me and hence not in the least interested in the ideas that I am trying out. But, in the main, I personally am interested only in comparatively small audiences and write not for the man in the street but for the man, figuratively speaking, in the automobile. He alone seems to me to be worthwhile. I should very much rather exchange ideas with one such man than with a thousand rubberheels: I like to think that I pick my readers as I pick my friends and companions. I am fortunate enough not to have to depend upon critical writing for my livelihood. It doesn't matter to me whether it sells or doesn't sell—not in the slightest, honestly. I therefore can say what I please how I please and whenever I please. If people like it, I am happy. If they don't like it, they can lump it.

Since every man's personal philosophy is reflected in his critical writings, it is natural that such critical writings as reflect an unpopular personal philosophy should fail to meet the taste of those other critics and laymen whose own philosophy is to a considerable degree derived from wall mottoes and from the popular prejudices of the place and moment. I happen to look at life not exactly like many other men, and their vanity and profound conviction in the rightness of their own philosophies accordingly lead them to believe that anyone who is different from themselves is *ipso facto* either self-deluded or a downright faker.

155

Thus, when I say in all honesty that I have absolutely no wish to reform anyone or anything, that I have no desire to make converts, that I haven't any other wish in the world than to amuse myself with ideas that seem to me not without savor, and that there is, to my way of looking at it, a hedonism in the matter of metaphysics no less than a hedonism more material—when I say these things and write these things other men vouchsafe themselves a warm wink and observe that something, to put it mildly, is wrong with me. That something may, in good sooth, be wrong with me is quite possible; but the mere circumstance that something may be wrong with me surely does not make me a poser.

The majority always believes that the minority has a screw loose. God, and the lowliest of His boobs no less, are always on the side of the biggest battalions.

§ 2

The critic of culture, experience and sensitiveness knows just two sound standards of judgment, to wit: 1. Whatever interests me is good; and 2. Whatever doesn't interest me is not good. The critical technic of critics of the lesser school, on the other hand, runs thus: 1. Whatever is good interests me; and 2. Whatever is not good does not interest me.   The subtle difference between these criteria of appraisal is the signal difference between the two arms of criticism.

§ 3

It is not that the critic who writes lightly does not take his subject seriously; it is simply that, like a man with the woman he truly and deeply loves, his very seriousness makes him light-hearted, happy and gay.   Beauty makes idiots sad as it makes wise men merry.   Men laugh with the things and persons that are closest to their hearts.   But because the rank and file of critics believe that there is something wrong with the kind of critic who, understanding thoroughly a thing that they themselves do not so thoroughly understand, takes that thing with a pleasantly careless whistle and the jaunty, sauntering swing of a cane, the latter is looked on with disfavor, and favor bestowed instead upon the kind of critic who would wear a long face at a ladies' day in a coon Turkish Bath.   This is always the fate of a critic who knows his job so superlatively well that he can turn it inside out.   The ideal critic of the multitude is not such a critic, but rather one who knows only half of his job and who conceals his lack of knowledge of the other half by taking seriously what he does not know, and writing of it even more seriously.

157

§ 4

There is an indignation that springs from the head and an indignation that springs from the heart. When my critics charge me with indignation, they fail, I believe, to perceive the difference between the two. My feelings are never indignant; my mind occasionally is.

§ 5

I often notice, with what I hope is a pardonable degree of amusement, that among those critics who are most hostile to me and to what I write are a considerable number who very plainly are imitators of my own style and method of critical attack.

§ 6

I cannot entirely agree with those critics who inveigh against propaganda in art and who maintain that propaganda, having no place in art, ruins art in its presence. Great art, they contend, proves nothing, should seek to prove nothing, may prove nothing. Many of the world's masterpieces confound such critics. "Hamlet" proves that it is futile for men to fight destiny as "Macbeth" proves that evil thought and wrongdoing can profit no

158

man. "The Mikado" is veiled propaganda against certain British weaknesses and peccadillos, as are also "Iolanthe", "Pinafore" and "The Pirates of Penzance". Wagner wrote "Der Fliegende Holländer" to prove that musical criticism as it was practised in Dresden at the time was ridiculous: the opera is propaganda against all standpat criticism. Beethoven's Ninth was composed to prove that his old teacher, Albrechtsberger, was something of a hanswurst. It proved it; it still proves it. Cervantes wrote "Don Quixote", so he himself said, "to break down the vogue and authority of books of chivalry and to render abhorred of men the false and absurd stories contained in books of chivalry". There is social and political propaganda in Swift's "Gulliver's Travels", as there are political plea and argument in Shaw's finest play, "Cæsar and Cleopatra". What is the wonderful ceiling in the Sistine Chapel but Michelangelo's successful attempt to prove that sculptural drawing may, in decoration, be the superior of painting?

§ 7

Literary criticism, as practised in the journals of the Republic, never fails to regard with favor the author who has apparently devoted great energy, patience and pains to the acquisition of his materials. His treatment of these materials and his deductions from them, that is to say, the net result of his arduous labors, are a secondary consideration with the critics. The time he devoted to the work, the amount of assiduity he displayed, the sweat he poured into his book—these are what arouse the critics' admiration and praise. Four out of every five American critics of literature never fail to endorse any two-pound book. Nine out of every ten American critics of literature never fail to endorse any book that contains a glossary of at least fifteen pages and an index of at least twenty. Any book with two or three reference footnotes to a page is certain of an enthusiastic critical reception. The only other kind of book that is as invariably sure of endorsement is one which, whatever its contents, has a gilt top.

§ 8

All that is necessary to raise a piece of imbecility into what the mob regards as a piece of profundity is to lift it off the floor and put it on a platform. Half the things that are said from a pulpit or rostrum or stage would get their spokesmen the bum's rush if they enunciated them five feet nearer the sea level.

§ 9

Art is not helped and developed so much by criticism as by criticism of criticism.

§ 10

It is held to be the duty of criticism to grant to the artist whatever thematic materials he chooses and to concern itself alone with the use which he makes of them. This, no doubt, is an excellent critical rule, and one that looks very well in the text-books, but I confess that, so far as I am concerned, I am often a poor critic when it comes to it. The thematic materials that an artist choses are, to me, almost as much a criticism of him as the achievement he distils from them. The difference between an artist and an artisan is the difference between the thematic materials of, say, "L'Aiglon" on the one hand and "In Old Kentucky" on the other. It is difficult to conceive of a Hauptmann starting off with the thematic materials of "Alias Jimmy Valentine" or a Zola with the thematic materials of "Pollyanna". It is easy enough, of course, to stick a thumb into the textual materials that genius has made use of and to show that they are intrinsically not far removed from claptrap—to show, indeed, that they are entirely similar to the textual materials used by ignoble

161

hands—but for every such proof that the materials of "The Comedy of Errors", for example, and those of some such pot-boiler as "Her Bridal Night" are at bottom alike, there are a dozen proofs that the textual materials an artist chooses are the mark of him. An artist would not be likely to choose, as a starting point, the thematic materials of "Nellie, the Beautiful Cloak Model", or "Brown of Harvard", or "Up in Mabel's Room". Nor is it likely that a hack would choose, as a starting point, the thematic materials of "Androcles and the Lion", or "The Last Night of Don Juan", or, to come down a hundred pegs, even "Liliom".

§ 11

In the fact that there has never been a first-rate artist who has recognized his best work as his best work lies one of the *raisons d'être* of criticism. Criticism has taught and encouraged first-rate artists their first-rateness, as it has taught and discouraged tenth-rate artists their tenth-rateness.

§ 12

The peruser of the art of criticism as it is currently exercised in our daily and weekly gazettes becomes steadily conscious of the fact that there has arisen a body of *clichés* with which that criti-

162

cism answers those persons whose work and ideas do not happen to meet with its approval. There was a time, in the history of even this daily and weekly criticism, when its adverse criticism was based upon at least a measure of understanding of the point of view it championed and upon a sufficient familiarity with the other side of the question to make its adverse comment at once comprehensible and fair. Today, however, there is small disposition to box the other man's viewpoint with any degree of intelligence or honesty. A study of such criticism reveals neither this intelligence nor honesty; it reveals, further, neither a tonic ridicule nor a sharp and devastating irony; it reveals, further still, neither the faculty for a good healthy horse-laugh nor a whacking and explosive slapstick. It tries to kill off its opponent by childish and inane means. It employs the tactics of the kindergarten. Thus, when it finds itself at a loss as to sound destructive criticism, it invariably falls back upon such recriminatory stencils as "So-and-so reminds one of a small boy drawing caricatures with a piece of chalk on the school-house fence" or "One cannot expect a man like So-and-so to understand the principles by which the rest of us are guided". The word "tradition" similarly looms large in the species of criticism of which I am speaking. Whenever one of these critics doesn't accurately know what is wrong with an opponent's point of view, save that it seems to him to be wrong, he takes refuge in imputing it either to the other man's traditions or lack of them. Again, we hear endless whiffle about "bad boys"—a bad boy, apparently, being anyone who doesn't believe exactly what the commentator concerned believes, and about "disrespectful attitude toward his elders", as if respect for age were an article in the doctrine of sound criticism. More and more, in this daily and weekly criticism, a man's ideas and performances are criticized less from the viewpoint of their honest worth and importance than from their adherence to or departure from the punctilio of the place and moment. Manners are rated above merit. A suave and poiseful nincompoop is regarded as the superior of a rough and forceful intelligence. The battle is not one of sound sense or effective seltzer-siphons; the battle is one in which the critic seeks to confound and put to rout his opponent with magpie rubber-stamps.

§ 13

The wisest morsel of criticism that I have heard in a long time came recently from the estimable Stokowski, of the Philadelphia Orchestra. Observed the estimable Stokowski, upon negotiating a palatable *Hahnenschwanz,* "To the hyenas with all these critics who are trying to teach people to understand music! Why should people understand music? It is enough that they love it!"

§ 14

Once we have laughed at a thing, it ceases in the future to be aught but food for laughter. I doubt if even a heaven-sent genius could today make us take seriously the theme of "Charley's Aunt", or cubist painting, or the point of view of American criticism during the late war.

§ 15

More than any other form of criticism is that concerned with drama subject to the enthusiasm of the moment; more than any other form is it influenced, whether intentionally or not, by more or less immediate comparisons. The best and worst dramatic critics are alike in this; neither can resist entirely the hypnotic eye of a similar play that has preceded the one which they are reviewing, or of a dramatist whose antecedent work makes the presently considered dramatist seem relatively good or bad, or of an actor or actress who has played the present rôle in the past, or of a half dozen other

165

such phenomena. It is thus that we must account, in part, for the otherwise somewhat puzzling enthusiasms of an Archer for a Pinero, of a Huneker for a Maeterlinck, or of a Shaw, in a measure, for a Barrie. And it is thus that we do account, on the whole, for lesser critics' enthusiasms—and megrims no less—over nine-tenths of the things about which they suffer enthusiasms or megrims.

§ 16

The position of the critic is a more or less delicate one. So long as he keeps strictly to his profession, he may give issue to even the most abysmal dooflickus in the way of critical opinion and get away with it. He is protected in such circumstances by all the old and largely senseless bywords such as "Every man has a right to his own opinion", "De gustibus non est disputandum", "There are two sides to every question", and the like. But when the critic ventures further to posture himself as a novelist, dramatist or what not, the delicacy of his position may be said to approach closely to the condition of a midwife *enceinte*. If the critic happens to be a genius, he may do all this and come triumphantly off the battlefield with the scalps, flags, service medals and underwear of his scoffers. But if the critic does not happen to be precisely a genius, he is likely to come off the field with an ear gone and his shirt-tail hanging out.

§ 17

It is doubtless one of my deficiencies as a prac-tising critical Magus that I do not care to see a play, however august a masterpiece it may be, acted time and again. After I have seen it played twice, or maybe three times, I am finally done with it, and to be asked to see it played still again I can only regard as foul innuendo against my talents and equipment. A fine play may conceivably be sus-ceptible of more than one interpretation, but it surely isn't susceptible of more than *three*. And to be bidden to see it performed at regular inter-vals is simply to be invited to waste one's valuable time watching various troupes of mummers earn a living. The critic who can't gather an intelligent opinion about a play after studying a single per-formance of it—and perhaps in certain cases studying the manuscript either before or after he sees it acted—has a tile loose somewhere. A sound opinion on acting may be achieved by weigh-ing different performances and making compari-sons, but a sound opinion on drama is achieved by the unit system. The man who has to go to "Hamlet" several times to convince himself that it is a first-rate play is the kind of man who would have to go to "Abie's Irish Rose" an equal number of times to make up his mind finally that it was a tenth-rate one. The masterpieces of drama are repeated endlessly not for cultured theatrical audiences, but for the uncultured and the cultural climbers. They are repeated year in and year out in the playhouse as one plus one equals two is repeated year in and year out in the kindergarten, and to the same end.

The quality of pleasure that a cultivated man gets from seeing a good play acted time and again is not dissimilar to that which a popinjay gets from hearing a dozen or more women repeat to him the words "I love you". While it is obvious that one may hear the same piece of fine music played time on end with rich æsthetic profit, it is—or at least it should be—equally obvious that the same thing fails to hold true of drama, and for a plain reason. Music is all the various moods a hearer brings to it; drama is the single mood a dramatist brings to his hearers. Haydn's "Creation" may mean a hundred different things to a hundred different intelligent and cultivated men, but Ibsen's "Doll's House" can mean only one thing to each and all of these same men. To read many meanings into such a drama is the diversion of dunderheads.

ATTITUDE TOWARD CRITICISM

The objection to this point of view wields a two-sided bilbo. First, we are told that a true work of art never grows tiresome, however often it be seen or listened to. This information has a pretty sound, but it contains also a considerable rasher of nonsense. Apply a simple test. Would the greatest admirer of "Œdipus Rex", for example, care to see it played once a week? Or once every six weeks? Or once every three months? Or once every six months? Or once, regularly, each year? Or would anyone, however highly he esteemed it, care to hear Schubert's symphony in C major or Beethoven's in C minor with unremitting regularity? If the answer is yes, then all I can say is that one of us is a liar. It is, in point of paradoxical fact, the particular and peculiar merit of a work of art that it grows tiresome more quickly than a work of dubious quality. This is because a true work of art is so complete, so towering in beauty and so thoroughly impressive in its majesty that, by its sheer bulk and size, it exhausts one. One gets tired of looking at the Alps where one can look year in and year out with charmed comfort at the rolling hills of England. When a person leaves the theatre after seeing, say, Strindberg's "The Father" or von Hofmannsthal's "Elektra" or Gorki's "Night Refuge" or Hauptmann's "The Weavers", he is tuckered out, spiritually,

169

emotionally, mentally—and often, one fears, physically. The dramatist has fashioned a complete circle: there is nothing left undone. He has given his auditor everything. He has taken him and squeezed him dry. But when the same person leaves the theatre after seeing, say, a Pinero or a Henry Arthur Jones play, he carries with him fully half his faculties still untouched and unsatisfied. A lot of room still remains within him for a dramatist to fill. Any honest man will agree that, while he cannot possibly conceive of going to "Iphigenia at Aulis" or to "Faust" two nights in succession, it is conceivable that he might go two nights in succession to something like "Is Zat So?" The man one finds standing day in and day out before Raphael's "Disputà" is either a schoolmaster or an art dealer, or the janitor.

A second argument is to the effect that, in the case of a dramatic masterpiece, one may enjoy repetition on the ground that this repetition affords actors, directors and scenic artists the opportunity for experiment in interpretation. Although this is undoubtedly true, I can't see but that this experimentation isn't the very thing that presently contributes most largely to one's mood of ennui. I have, in more than twenty years of professional sitting, seen but three fine plays differently, yet intelligently, interpreted by different actors. All the

other fine plays that have been revived have either
been slaughtered to the vanity of idiotic actors'
theories of interpretation or have shown no dis-
cernible advance in acting over that vouchsafed
them in their earlier presentations. So far as direction goes, all that we have got, with a few not-
able exceptions, has been an intrinsically silly
hocus-pocus with expensive lighting apparatus and
inexpensive but rationally costly text rearrange-
ments. And in the matter of stage decoration,
when you say Gordon Craig you say "Amen".
There are those who believe that a dramatic masterpiece is given a new lease of life every time some
enterprising young man thinks up a freakish way to
interpret it and put it on, but didoes of this sort generally chloroform the masterpiece so far as I am
concerned. The "Medea" that I know isn't helped
any by producing it on the musicless merry-go-
round known as the Drehbühne, nor is "The Master
Builder" steinached by playing it as if it were "It
Pays To Advertise". Revivals conducted after
such plans are less for cultured audiences than for
such audiences as find pleasure and profit in watching vaudeville acrobats negotiate new and strange
flip-flops or Houdini escape from a newly devised
and exceptionally intricate garbage can. All the
actors and directors in the world haven't made a
Shakespearian masterpiece a whit more beautiful

than it was, I venture, in the crude theatrical day of Elizabeth. And it is thus I say that the man who relishes seeing a fine play a half dozen or a dozen times is the man who isn't able thoroughly to understand it, appreciate it and revel in it the first time he sees it. The cross-word puzzle was invented by the fellow who constantly finds new, hidden meanings in "Peer Gynt".

§ 18

That personal friendships influence criticism is a platitude beside the whiskers of which those of the M. Hughes look like maiden-hair fern. If there was ever a critic who was not held back from a completely honest appraisal of a friend, his finger-prints remain to be taken by the beadles. But personal friendship is not the only thing that influences and checks absolutely forthright critical assaying and evaluation. There are others. A polite, humorous and engaging letter from one whose work has previously not met with one's approval; an act performed with philosophical courage in the face of violent majority opposition which happens to echo one's own attitude and hence arouses one's respect and admiration; a serious and miserable illness, news of which has come to the critic's ear; an article by the criticized praising the virtues of the critic in intelligent terms and yet without a suspicion of flattery—these also often contrive in a measure to tie the hands of criticism. Thoroughly honest and uninfluenced criticism is possible only to a critic who lives alone on top of an Alp. And even then, let the manufacturer of his hot-water bag write a novel, and watch the result!

§ 19

It is not criticism that the loudest yodelers against criticism object to, but the printing of criticism. Oral criticism, though it be exactly like the published criticism, you will find they don't in the least object to. It is criticism set down in black and white that disquiets them. The average man, called a *lausbub'* by another man, simply laughs it off with genial unconcern. But the moment the other man calls him a *lausbub'* in print, he gets hot under the collar.

XI. ATTITUDE TOWARD THE KU KLUX KLAN

Not a single sound reason has yet been advanced for putting the Ku Klux Klan out of business. If the Klan is against the Catholics, so are the Masons. If the Klan is against the Jews, so are half of the good hotels of the Republic and three-quarters of the good clubs. If the Klan is against the foreign-born or hyphenated citizen, so is the National Institute of Arts and Letters. If the Klan is against the Negro, so are all of the States south of the Mason-Dixon line. If the Klan is for damnation and persecution, so is the Methodist Church. If the Klan is bent upon political control, so are the American Legion and Tammany Hall. If the Klan wears grotesque uniforms, so do the Knights of Pythias and the Mystic Shriners. If the Klan holds its meetings in the dead of night, so do the Elks. If the Klan conducts its business in secret, so do all of the college Greek letter fraternities and the Department of State. If the Klan holds idiotic parades in the public streets, so do the police, the letter-carriers and the firemen. If the Klan's officers bear ridiculous names, so do the officers of the Lambs' Club. If the Klan uses the mails for shaking down suckers, so does the Red Cross. If the Klan constitutes itself a censor of private morals, so does the Congress of the United States. If the Klan lynches a Moor for raping someone's daughter, so would you or I.

Yet the death rattle of the Klan, presaging the early demise of that Grand Order of the Facial Diaper, becomes increasingly audible and so brings the student of public phenomena to the business of contemplating the contributory causes. The most popular reason assigned for the *dégringolade* is that the order has been gradually ridiculed out of court. Nothing, it is said, can stem the tide of ridicule. And it has been such ridicule in the form of thousands of cartoons and caricatures and lampoons, thousands of wheezeful editorials, the swish of Ma Ferguson's red flannel petticoat, the nose-fingerings of countless stage comiques, the newspaper accounts of innumerable Klan parades and demonstrations that have been broken up by a lone-handed Irish cop, and similar seltzer-siphon sprayings that has, it is claimed, made the Klan a laughing stock.

That this is the actual reason for the Klan's steady loss of strength and position, however, I

175

privilege myself to doubt. Ridicule, it is true, is a powerful weapon, but its power is infinitely less great in These States than elsewhere. Many local personages and institutions of varying degrees of integrity and merit have withstood its onslaughts effectively. Ridicule never hurt Doctor Munyan, or Lydia Pinkham, or the *Police Gazette*, or General Dawes, or the Theatrical Syndicate, or Mrs. Winslow, or the cheap sex magazines, or Henry Ford, or Oshkosh, or Eleanor H. Porter, or jazz bands, or Mayor Hylan, or the Elks, or Henry Cabot Lodge, or Billy Sunday, or Chauncey Depew, or a hundred like them. They have all got fat and thrived on it. It has made them rich and famous and happy. Similarly, the Klan could withstand ridicule to the end of its days and prosper in the midst of the thickest bombardment of custard tarts. Ridicule, unless I am in sorry error, has had nothing to do with tying a can to the Klan. What has contrived to give the Klan the adieu kiss is, rather, the opposite. For every American who has bestowed a derisory hoot upon the Exalted Order of the Nocturnal Chemise, there have been fifty or more who have taken it soberly and seriously. For one who has ridiculed it, there have been many, many more who have regarded it with emotions akin to fear and trembling. And it is this, paradoxically enough, that

176

has sent it to its present sick-bed. The reason
should be obvious. For all the altiloquent dec-
larations of noble purpose on the part of the Klan's
bosses, the rank and file of the Klan's members
are in the thing less to keep the United States safe
from democracy than to have a good time. Just
as a college boy joins a Greek letter fraternity infinitely less to promote the moral, ethical and
philosophical teachings of Aristotle, Socrates,
Plato, Xenophon, Alcibiades—or whatever other
Greek happens to be the tutelary saint of the order
—among the twenty-five other boys in the fraternity
house than to become chummy with a number of
companionable souls who will join him in midnight keg parties, secret trips to New York to see
the "Follies", and Saturday night expeditions to
Dutch Rosie's just outside the town limits, just so
do the majority of young men join the Klan chiefly
for the sport and amusement it will vouchsafe
them. The Klan may be founded spiritually on
a plane of lofty purposes and endeavors, but its
potential success, materially, financially and every
other way, was founded on the universal impulse
of every young man to get a chance to kick up his
heels once in a while in some otherwise forbidden
manner. The white hood and night-shirt offered
young men this chance, and they took it. And it
offered them not only this chance for an occasional

lark; it offered them also and coincidently a bit of romance and glamor and mystery in the negotiation of that lark.

For a while, then, all was well and the Klan prospered. But gradually the Klan began to feel the effects of its serious reception by the country at large. This, of course, was by no means displeasing to the chiefs and sachems of the *bund*, but it was anything but pleasing to a very considerable number of the privates in the ranks. These gentlemen, the most of them clerks, office-boys, small-town post-masters, delivery wagon drivers and such, who had joined up purely out of a spirit of simple adventure—akin to reading a Nick Carter or Diamond Dick paper-back—now found that they were getting more than they had bargained for. They had joined a Social and Pleasure Club and now suddenly found themselves members of a Factor in National Politics. They had paid in twelve dollars and a half to indulge in a jolly Hallowe'en Night carnival the year 'round only to discover that they were a National Menace and a whole lot of other such irrelevant and irritating delicatessen. And it all began to seem damfoolish to them—and excessively disappointing. They had started out on a chowder party and clambake, with Catholics and Jews for the chowder and some very appetizing dinges for clams, and had ended up, it appeared, several miles from their gala destination—in the rain. The sardonic humor of the thing struck them— even them, clerks, office-boys and dray-drivers though they were. And they began to feel a trifle sheepish and dog-faced, and vastly uncomfortable. Self-ridicule, though perhaps unidentified as such to their own senses, began to assail them. And the Klan began to hit the greased toboggan. It was given the push not by popular ridicule, but by ridicule from within. Nothing in the world— no man, no organization, no institution—can face that and live.

But if error creeps into these calculations and if, indeed, the Klan is destined to survive, it must be advised and encouraged by all other 100 per cent Americans who wish patriotically to preserve 100 per cent Americanism. From a bulletin recently issued by the Department of the Interior, Bureau of Education, on "Flag Exercises for the Schools of the Nation", I therefore quote for the Klan a list of foreign-born Americans whose average percentage, by the current standard of American weights and measures, is perhaps not greater than 35, and who hence—were they still living—would be fair prey for a tar and feather

179

THE AUTOBIOGRAPHY OF AN ATTITUDE

massage: James J. Hill, John Singer Sargent, Albert Gallatin, Augustus Saint-Gaudens, Carl Schurz, Louis Agassiz, John Ericsson, Frederick William Steuben, Franz Sigel, Alexander Hamilton . . .

XII. ATTITUDE TOWARD ENGLAND AND THE ENGLISH

§ 1

Of all men, the Englishman is the only one whose patriotism has about it an air of dignity. The Englishman loves his country in the way that a man loves a patient, faithful and sympathetic woman to whom he has been married for years on end and whose life with her has been replete with comfort and peace. The Frenchman, on the other hand, loves his country as he would a gaudy chorus nymph whose anatomy had fascinated him; the German, his, as a sophomore loves his college football team; and the American, his, as Jumbo loved Barnum.

§ 2

There is always this difference, I find, between the Englishman and the American. I have known many Americans who would not mind living in England, but I have never yet found an Englishman who said he would care to live in the United States.

§ 3

The armies of England and America may fight shoulder to shoulder; the diplomats of England and America may stand side by side in their uplifting of the world; the two navies may salute each other with constant salvos of cannon; the two governments may be as Siamese twins—but it all does not and will not amount to a damn unless the average Englishman can soon train himself to be less patronizing to the average American when he serves him his Stilton cheese or sells him a shirt.

§ 4

On its upper level, contemporary English criticism is eminently sound, fair and honorable. But on its middle and lower levels there is no more contemptible criticism being written in the world today. In its attitude toward everything American is this latter criticism especially disgusting. In the place of reason, it offers merely condescension; in the place of judgment and honest appraisal, it offers only superior sneers. It views American literature, American drama and American taste with deliberately bilious and squinting eyes. It is, in aspect, like a clerk whining enviously because of his boss' good fortune.

182

§ 5

Of the many varieties of *Homo sapiens,* the civilized Englishman makes perhaps the most agreeable companion. He is freer from objectionable nonsenses than the man of any other nationality. His manners are more pleasant, his conversation is more cosmopolitan, his tastes are more in accordance with one's own than a Frenchman's or German's or American's or any one's else. He is more intelligently amiable; he is a better drinking partner; he is less given to prejudice, indignation, moral intensity, bosh. This, of course, is true only of the worldly and educated Britisher. His fellow countryman of a lower level is a jake most sour.

§ 6

The mere mention of Limehouse brings the picture vividly before one's eyes. Soft-footed, slinky Chinese peering out of dark doorways; cut-throats, their faces half concealed with mufflers, their caps pulled down over sinister eyes, lurking in the shadows of ominous alleys; fitful lights from dingy upper stories hinting at evil; opium dens, their bunks full of the waste of white womanhood and sailors from the seven seas; mulattoes, East Indians, convicts escaped via the trading ships up

183

from the Congo, scheming Orientals, drug barter-
ers, murderers in hiding from the police—a pan-
orama of crouching wickedness, scarlet sin, peril
and jeopardy. A plague-spot of infinite, quiver-
ing romance and mystery, of danger a-tremble and
ever ready to spring, of hushed and nervous ma-
lignity, made famous the world over by the tales
of Thomas Burke, the "Broken Blossoms" of D.
W. Griffith, the paragraphs of a hundred journal-
ists, and the scenes in stage melodramas without
end.

One night in London recently a British friend
waxed hotly enthusiastic over Limehouse, and over
Burke's and Griffith's celebration of it. "I tell
you", he exclaimed, "there's nothing so spectacu-
larly, so uncannily evil in all Europe as Limehouse! The very feel of dark crime hovers over
the place. The romance of unexplored mystery
is in the very air". And so on for three more
whiskeys and soda.

My comparative coolness, my failure to share in
his ecstasy, presently irritated him. He bade the
reason for my indifference.

"You will recall", I said, "a quotation by your
Bernard Shaw from a German novel in which a
crowd of medieval warriors, fired by the eloquence
of Peter the Hermit, burns with a Christian longing to rush to the Holy Land and charge in ser-

ried ranks on the Paynim hosts—all except one man, who is obviously not impressed. Indignant at his coldness, they demand what he means by it. 'I've been there', is his sufficient explanation". I, also, had been to Limehouse.

About a week before the above conversation I had suggested to another English friend of mine a midnight trip to the notorious den of iniquity. He set the night. "I suppose", I said, "that we'd better rig ourselves up for the expedition. Old clothes, a slouch hat and so on, I venture, the better to avoid attracting undue attention?"

"Old fellow, the better to avoid attracting attention", he replied, "we had best stick to the conventional dinner jacket".

It was along about half-past eleven of a Friday night, after an excellent dinner, a quart of champagne and an act and a half of the "Charlot Revue" that we arrived in that area beyond Stepney Station and in the neighborhood of the West India Dock Road that is known as Limehouse. I may perhaps best and most quickly convey a first impressionistic view of Limehouse by saying that it looks something like Hoboken, New Jersey, save that the streets are not so dirty. But this fact did not entirely reassure me. My qualms were doubtless visible in my expression. "No need for caution", my friend rallied me. "The only danger to life and limb down here in Limehouse is from the crowd of sightseers". Even as he spoke, I fell back and uttered a hoarse cry of pain. Someone had stepped on my foot. I looked up. It was Lee Shubert.

We were, my friend and I, soon in the heart of the district. While not so well lighted as Broadway, say, it was quite as brightly illuminated as West Fifty-ninth Street. That is, all of it save three small, crooked alleys. These we determined to have a look at first. In one, two bobbies —the only human beings observable—were lazily sneaking a few puffs at their pipes and discussing the Ascot races. In a second, four little boys, cunning English youngsters, were playing the game we Americans know as mumble-t'e-peg. In the third, a gentle-faced Spitz dog was proving that he was house-broken.

"But where," I demanded, "are all the cut-throats and murderers?"

"Some blocks away", replied my friend, "in jail".

An evil-looking Chinaman approached us. As he came nearer, I observed that he had on a Troy, N. Y., collar and what was unmistakably a re-versible necktie. The fellow edged toward my friend and whispered something under his breath. Alarmed for my friend's safety, I stepped quickly to his side and seized my cane tightly, prepared to use it upon the villainous Oriental's head should necessity arise.

"No need", observed my friend. "This"—he turned to me as the Chinaman grinned and held out his hand—"is Ching Lee. Everybody knows Ching. He used to be Rupert Brooke's valet. He's now working for a fellow by the name of Moe Greenblatt, who is in the guide business. Ching is one of the guides that Moe has assigned to Limehouse. He says that for three shillings he will show us something very tasty".

We hired Ching, who, after considerable hocus-pocus that included much shushing and tiptoeing —he confessed to us later that this had always impressed Thomas Burke—led us up two creaky flights of stairs in a rickety-looking dwelling to a room about twelve feet square. This room had bunks along the walls, was lighted by a single dirty oil lamp and smelled generally like an eager glue factory. In one of the bunks lay a sailor, smoking a long pipe. In another sprawled a fat woman, also puffing at a long pipe.

"Opium den!" triumphantly exclaimed Ching.

We sniffed the air. We looked at each other. We nodded. What the "sailor" and the fat gal ("Bad, bad woman", so Ching described her) were smoking was—unless nostrils of long training deceived us—good old Virginia fine-cut.

"But surely", I protested as we regained the street, "there must be scarlet women in Lime-house, poor girls who have been kidnapped and led into lives of shame!"

"I'll show you some of them. Come along!" returned my friend and quickly made off into a dim, winding passageway. At the end of the passageway was a small two-story frame building. We entered without knocking. A room with six wooden tables confronted us. Two were occupied by men and women drinking very pale beer. Two were unoccupied. At one of the others sat two women, one about thirty-five, the other about three years younger. They were dressed like prosperous Beaver Falls, Pa., servant girls. At the remaining table sat a girl alone—like the two others drinking the pale, watery beer. She was about twenty-five or so.

"Let's sit down and talk to her", whispered my friend. "She may be one of the poor kidnapped girls you spoke of".

We sat down—she did not protest—and ordered three more beers from the affable host and servitor. His name, we discovered later, was Gustav Wenz and he had been, before Prohibition stalked the American scene, a waiter at Lüchow's in Fourteenth Street, New York. It was not long after we had sat down that we learned that our fair companion, the poor kidnapped maiden of my imagination, was none other than the amiable Gustav's estimable wife and the mother of his little son Hugo. We moved to the other table.

Here, after four rounds of the peroxide lager, we became privy to the information that the elder of the "girls" was employed at eight shillings a night to sit around and give the place an "air", and that the younger was a cousin of hers who worked in the misses' waists department at Selfridge's.

Coming out of the passageway—it had grown a bit foggy—we bumped into two peculiarly vicious looking individuals. Again I laid tight hold of my walking stick, prepared to ward off any dastardly attack from these denizens of the underworld. Murderers, garroters, Jack-the-Rippers and worse, perhaps. Suddenly one of them reached out and grabbed my arm. The other as promptly grabbed my other arm. They let out a yell. One was Sinclair Lewis and the other was Paul Whiteman.

Other denizens of Limehouse that my friend and I encountered that night—all were in the conventional evening clothes save Al Woods, who boasts that he hasn't worn a boiled shirt since he lost an election bet on Benjamin Harrison—included John Drinkwater, Florence Mills, Frank Crowninshield, Condé Nast, Irene Castle, Gilbert Miller, Albert De Courville, Cornelius Vanderbilt Whitney, Professor James C. Hemmingway, wife and children, Paul DeKruif, late of the Rockefeller Institute, Marie Dressler, Dorothy Dickson, Georges Carpentier, the Six Morgan Dancers, Hermann Oelrichs, George Robey, Philip Guedalla, George Doran, Professor Frederick Jameson, Mr. and Mrs. Louis Archibald Evans and daughter Hilda, of Topeka, Kansas, Ray Goetz, Irving Berlin, Arthur C. Verney, of the Cleveland, Ohio, Y. M. C. A., Arthur Bingham Walkley, Henri Béraud, of the *Mercure de France*, J. C. Squire, Mr. and Mrs. Alvin Peabody Sampson and son Peter, of Altoona, Pa., Mr. Marx, of Hart, Schaffner and Marx, the Lee Kids with their mother, Hugh Walpole, William Randolph Hearst, Elsie Janis and Ma Janis, Vincent Astor, Joe Flinn, of the Famous Players Company, Count Arpad Ferenczi and the Countess, the Reverend Doctor Ambrose Worthington of the Millsboro, Delaware, First M. E. Church, Will Vodery, A. A. Milne, T. S. Eliot, and Mr. and Mrs. James Finch and children, of Los Angeles, California.

"There" exclaimed my friend abruptly, indicating a half-caste slouching in a doorway, "is Nigger Blake, as he is known—the most picturesque character in all Limehouse!"

"Who is he? What has he done?" I asked, breathless.

"He earns a living acting as a super in the movies whose scenes are laid in Limehouse", my friend answered, adjusting his monocle. "His real name is Morris Feldman. He used to run a small clothing shop in Tottenham Court Road, but failed. Unable to make a living, he hit on the idea of dressing himself up as you see him, loafing around Limehouse and waiting until the movie people came snooping around for atmosphere. As 'atmosphere' he rents himself out and often makes as much as five pounds a week".

"But", I asked in despair, "isn't there anywhere such a thing as a real Limehouse?"

"Only", replied my friend, "in the pages of fiction".

§ 7

Rural England is so still and quiet and peaceful that it always seems to the stranger as if the folk of the country were off fighting some great war.

§ 8

English flowers are as formal as Englishmen themselves. There is nothing nonchalant, nothing free and easy about them, as with the flowers of other countries. They are stiff, erect, immobile. They are England.

§ 9

London is the bachelor capital of the world. It combines the hard philosophy of Berlin with the gentle charm of Paris.

§ 10

No man has seen London who hasn't seen its dawn.

§ 11

There are more valets in London than there are trousers.

§ 12

The virtue of every Englishman is that he is able to convince one that he is a gentleman even in such cases as he isn't.

192

§ 13

London gets the better-grade American traveler. Paris gets the rest.

§ 14

The Englishman makes virtues of those things that the American is pleased to regard as vices.

§ 15

The Englishman is well-mannered; the Frenchman, polite.

§ 16

The Englishman assumes that the American is his equal. The latter soon convinces him, however, that the American is his inferior.

§ 17

England is a democracy in perfectly fitting evening clothes.

§ 18

One notices that those Englishmen who are most contemptuous of the American's regard for money are all over here lecturing their heads off.

§ 19

One of my books was recently published in England. I observe that it has been highly praised by those English critics who like America and Americans and vigorously damned by those who do not like America and Americans. The book itself, so far as I am able to make out, has been dealt with by only one man.

§ 20

The Englishman: "I have met Thomas Hardy".
The American: "I have met the Mountbattens".

§ 21

England, Home and Beauty.—Bushy Park, dark and cool green under its peristyle of ancient oaks, on a still and lazy mid-June afternoon, the cows munching the grass beyond the distant lake, in the foreground a little girl seated on a bench reading "Alice in Wonderland", and from far, far off down the road the faint echo of a coaching horn . . . the Embassy Club in Bond Street brilliant at midnight, with the band playing a swinging tune and the young Prince of Wales, his arm around a fair partner, amiably bumping his foxtrot way through the dancing crowds . . . Piccadilly Circus at ten o'clock of a misty, rainy evening with the colored electric signs taking on the aspect of so many melted opals . . . Rotten Row at eleven in the springtime morning, with its sleek young English girls astride glistening horses, galloping past benches filled with wide-eyed children and their governesses . . . mid-day brandy in the little Tour Eiffel beside the great shining brass palm pots . . . the taxicab jams in Trafalgar Square with the miraculous escapes from death every other minute by the crippled vendors of newspapers and the old women selling flowers . . . London Bridge the moment before the hush of the breaking dawn . . . the tapestry of yellow blossoms that covers the fields on the roads to the southland . . . the Ritz at the cocktail hour with its migratory Argentinians searching hither and thither in quest of beauty, and with each cocktail served by three waiters . . . the Blue Lagoon at three in the morning . . . the solitary, lonely lamp at the end of the dim little passageway known as St. James's Place . . . the cries of "Strawberries!" in the London streets by day and of "Roses!" in the London streets by night . . . the match slot-machine in the bar of the Regent Theatre up Euston Road that marks the Prohibition division line after ten o'clock, to the left of which drinks may be served and to the right of which they mayn't . . . the Thames on Ascot Sunday with its moving picture of white flannel trousers and lavender skirts . . . the famous Trooping of the Color, all gold and scarlet and crashing music, with a small boy, his hand in his mother's, blowing a kiss with his other to the Queen of England . . .

XIII. ATTITUDE TOWARD EUROPE AND EUROPEANS

§ 1

French wines have made more converts for France than French diplomacy.

§ 2

The European powers have not been able to fetch the Turk with bullets, so now they are going after him with morals.

§ 3

Switzerland is the one country in the world that has never risen superior to its geography. Take away its mountains and all that is left is a New Jersey, full of cheese.

§ 4

The Bulgarian is the lounge-lizard of European politics.

§ 5

The Italian never thinks.   He leaves thinking to his enemies.   In this he is sagacious and extremely wise.   One by one his enemies think themselves into dire difficulties and so relieve him of going to all the trouble himself.

§ 6

The Frenchman is the Irishman of continental Europe.

§ 7

The Spaniard is the laziest man in Europe. And why not?   What is there for him to do or to worry about?

§ 8

The Irish are Germans suffering from spontaneous combustion.

§ 9

The trouble with the French is that they knew Potsdam but not Munich.

§ 10

It is the German's tragedy that he knows how to handle a gun, but not a diplomat.

§ 11

Bismarck's greatness lay in the masterly greatness of his errors. Kaiser Wilhelm's pettiness lay in the masterly pettiness of his triumphs.

§ 12

One should see Paris only the first time.

XIV. ATTITUDE TOWARD THE DRAMA

§ 1

When a playwright, instead of viewing his subject matter conventionally in the theatrical sense, views it conventionally in the non-theatrical sense, the procedure inevitably gives issue to what the theatre knows as an intelligent play, which is to say a play that views its subject matter in the way that the average and not overly intelligent lime and cement dealer views it. A grain of any kind of intelligence always seems like a bombshell in the theatre. What the theatre calls for is not forthright perception and intelligence but only such minor elements in forthright perception and intelligence as lend themselves to an easily assimilable show.

§ 2

The dramatist cannot afford to be too truthful. The public ever demands a measure of compromise with truth. It wants its truth in small doses and its illusions in large. It may, for argument's sake, be willing to grant, somewhat reluctantly, that man is descended from the monkey and that two plus two equals four, but it demands in return for these admissions that it be assured that there is a pot of gold at the end of the rainbow, that Joan of Arc was a virgin, that a belief in God will cure fallen arches, and that the spirit of one's late grandfather is ready at all times to show up in a black velvet cabinet and play a tambourine solo.

§ 3

It is the belief of the American playwright who sets out to write what is known as a drawing-room comedy that all he has to do to achieve his end is to write a vulgar farce and have it played in half-time in a set painted a soft gray and furnished tastefully by one of the fashionable Madison Avenue shops. The only things that differentiate one of these so-called polite drawing-room comedies from an impolite rural comedy are several pretty lamps, an appropriate number of dinner jackets, a portly English actor in the rôle of a butler, a baby-grand piano with an expensive piece of embroidery thrown nonchalantly over one end, a dingus off-stage to imitate the sound of an automobile, and a stage director able to make the actors speak in well-modulated voices. Otherwise, for all that

201

it matters intrinsically, the average native-made drawing-room comedy might just as well be played in the kitchen.

The American who essays to write drawing-room comedy, even when he is moderately successful, gives one the impression of being altogether too conscious of his manners. The Englishman, even at his worst, in the same field of dramatic entertainment is casual and persuasive. But the American seems always to have thought up his good manners first and the rest of his play afterward. The manners flash out from the manuscript like so many goldfish in a barrel of dill-pickles. The characters comport themselves not easily and naturally, but like dollar books of etiquette in five-dollar bindings. The hero is just a half-inch too suave; the heroine is just a shade too elegant; the butler is just a touch too butlerish. One feels that the author rather than the audience is the one who is impressed.

The first essential in the writing of genuine polite comedy is that the author shall be sufficiently versed in the code of polite manners to be able safely to forget them when he writes his comedy. These polite manners must, so to speak, be felt but never seen. They should be the undertone and implication of the play, not the circus parade and overtone. The author must be so sure of his

202

ground that the punctilio, as the punctilio, shall be comfortably forgotten by the audience ten minutes after the first curtain has gone up and shall thereafter be taken for granted. It must never come into the foreground, as our American writers permit it to; it must remain ever lurking in the silken back shadows. When good manners are emphasized they cease to be good manners. What results is vulgarity.

§ 4

There perhaps never lived a dramatic actor who did not believe that if all the playwrights in the world were suddenly to be wiped out by cholera morbus he couldn't earn an equally handsome livelihood and reputation for himself by becoming a pantomimist. To the dramatic actor, pantomime approximates, in its major phases, the business of rolling off a log. It is something to be taken up casually, like buying a new pearl-gray derby hat or acting in a Samuel Shipman play. No training, no understanding, no experience are necessary; that is, no training, no understanding, and no experience that the actor does not already posses. If, forsooth, he is the brilliant fellow he is in the matter of triumphing over the nonsensical words these fool dramatists put into his mouth,

why shouldn't he be twice as brilliant if all this
spoken gibberish were got rid of and he be allowed to go it on his own?   Surely his face and
features are twice as expressive as Strindberg at
his utmost, surely his body, with or without the
aid of Wetzel or Kuppenheimer, can suggest more
drama than any of these upstart young O'Neills.
And what, pray, is pantomime but an actor let
loose on a stage and come into his rightful own,
without outside interference?   Pick out any actor who didn't lose a leg in the war or who, if he
did, is free from rheumatism in the other, and you
have a pantomimist!

This prevalent actor-notion that pantomime is
simply drama with the words left out is responsible
for the latter-day death of pantomime as a theatrical art.   For on such occasions as an attempt has
been made to reinterest the public in the silent
stage, what has been presented to the public has not
been pantomime at all in its real sense, but merely
bad drama interpreted by mute actors.   The result is obvious.   Instead of the drama of suggestion, which pantomime is, there has been disclosed
only a repertoire of the rubber-stamp mummer
gestures, chest-heavings, eye-rollings, fist-clench-
ings, shoulder-shruggings, etc., which invariably
accompany the spoken drama, minus the speeches
that the playwright vouchsafes the performers.

The pantomime that we have got, therefore, has been, with precious few exceptions, simply bad cinema acting. Just as some of the best dramatic actors have turned out to be bad moving-picture actors when they have attempted the screen and some of the best moving-picture actors have turned out to be bad dramatic actors when they have attempted the stage, so have some of the best dramatic actors turned out to be melancholy performers when they have attempted that combination of stage and screen that goes by the name of pantomime. These dramatic actors and actresses have bodies which are suggestive enough when their movements are glossed over, given point and helped along by the words of a playwright, but which are forlorn and lost when they are called on to rely entirely upon themselves. Such actors and actresses have not the bodies for pantomime any more than Little Egypt and La Belle Fatima have the minds for drama. They are able to suggest the rough outlines of the drama that inheres in pantomime, but the details and the shadings elude them completely. Their bodies flow against the current of the pantomime, not with it. The two do not mix. What we see are dramatic actors running around the outskirts of the pantomime, tagging it faintly now and then, but never being tagged, in turn, by it. And the pantomime that

205

thus comes to us in the final impression is little more than a crude moving picture thrown against the floor of a stage instead of against a white sheet.

Pantomime, as these dramatic performers evidently see it, is merely a matter of external movement. Such external movement, however, produces but the externals of pantomime, as the mere reading of the lines of a play at the first rehearsal produces only the externals of drama. I am not so foul an idiot as to say that pantomime requires a wealth of preliminary thinking out, a great antecedent reading of meanings into the movement of each muscle and toe-nail, but it surely calls for a considerable feeling out of its rôles. The dramatic actor must think out his rôle; the pantomimist must feel out his rôle. Drama is, very largely, a retailing of externals; pantomime, a retailing of internals. The dramatic actor, at his best, is the funnel of another's expressed mind; the pantomimist, at his best, is the funnel of another's unexpressed emotions.

§ 5

It is a common and generally successful dodge of the modern dramatist to treat what would ordinarily be comedy scenes seriously and what would ordinarily be dramatic scenes lightly. This device generally deceives the laymen, as well as many of the professional reviewers, into regarding as a work of art, and one blessed with what they call a fresh and original viewpoint, almost any play that employs it. These persons confuse a point of view of life with a point of view of dramatics. The clever playwright fools them into believing that he is an original dramatic thinker by the simple hocus-pocus of saying no where they anticipate that he will say yes and yes where they expect him to say no. The playwright in question first writes his play as the average Broadway or Shaftesbury Avenue playwright would have written it and then diplomatically converts it into a play that jounces the critics by the simple deception of changing all the tears into laughs and all the laughs into tears.

§ 6

In all of Bernard Shaw's work there are no finer passages than those which go to make up the last half of the last act of that comedy among modern comedies known as "Candida". I know of no better instance of intelligent sentimental writing. Taking materials that, these thirty years ago, were already deeply imbedded in the hokum of the popular theatre, Shaw converted them into first-grade dramatic literature by the simple device of viewing them through the eyes of the mind rather than through the eyes of the heart, as they had previously been in the custom of being viewed. The playwright of commerce is invariably given to an attempt to touch the heart through the heart. Shaw knew better. He knew that the shortest road to the human heart is through the head. Where the playwrights of his earlier day jockeyed with an audience's sentimental emotions with what may be called heart-to-heart drama, he made it his own trick to do the jockeying with mind-to-heart drama. It is the easiest thing in the world to instil in an audience's heart the mood of agreeable melancholy; but it is a difficult thing, indeed, to instil the same mood in an audience's head.

§ 7

The notion that it is time that has showed up the superficiality and spuriousness of the Pinero drama, that the years elapsed since its creation have been its most devastating critic, seems to me somewhat too complimentary to the genial Sir Arthur. While it is true that it has taken the general public some thirty years or so to discover that the Pinero plays which originally seemed to it to

be great masterpieces are intrinsically nothing but
third-rate social melodrama, about the only really
intelligent person who was fooled these threescore
years ago was our late estimable friend Archer.
Almost every other critic, professional or lay, who
was able to distinguish at all between the main-
spring of a watch and the time recorded by the
watch—that is, between mechanical proficiency
and the sentimental philosophical clickings of the
moment—appreciated the plays exactly for what
they were worth. A good play is a good play,
thirty years ago, today, and thirty years hence. A
poor play is always a poor play. Fashions in
speech, in dress, in manners and in other externals
may change, but true insight, true philosophy, true
perception never change. Of true insight, philosophy and perception Pinero has, and ever has had,
a minimum. That is why his drama, with precious little exception, has aged so rapidly into caricature. Take, for example, "The Second Mrs.
Tanqueray". (And what is said of it applies to
most of the others.) "Tanqueray", when it was
originally produced, was a popular success not because it was a good play, but because it was, at the
time, in the eyes of the generality of theatregoers,
a daring novelty. It succeeded in the early eighteen nineties for precisely the same reason that
such a play as "On Trial" has succeeded more re-

cently. It belongs not to that catalogue of the theatre which contains sound drama, but to that catalogue which contains tricky drama. It has, assuredly, been effective at the box-office, and it has also impressed profoundly the one-inch-deep emotionalism of two-feet-thick skulls, but so, too, have been effective in the same way "The White Heather", Lew Morrison's "Faust" and "Sawing a Woman in Two".

"Tanqueray" is, in good truth, pathetically feeble stuff. Even the much-vaunted perfection of its mechanical structure does not overly bewitch those of us who doubt that men are suddenly given to the writing of letters when they have friends in to dinner, that the inevitable and expected person always shows up at the right moment, that the crisis of one's life goes arm in arm with extravagant coincidence, and other such artless dramatic conveniences. Nor, despite meticulous English and neatly manœuvred phrases, are some of us stimulated by the kind of dramatic writing wherein, in moments of embarrassment, presumably adult and intelligent males fumble elaborately with cigars and coffee cups, wherein the same presumably adult and intelligent persons jump to their feet and, with glasses aloft, propose H. V. Esmond toasts to one another, wherein the same males (incidentally, Englishmen) indulge constantly in a deal of hearty and loving hand-shaking and shoulder-patting, and in which the humor consists wholly of such old Alhambra and Empire wheezes as are derived from allusions to pancakes, loud snorings, and a woman's being so cold that one gets chapped lips when one kisses her, to say nothing of such pleasantries as is-he-dead? well-it's-the-same-thing—he's-married, and of such old stage reliables as the comic drunk. Yet there is, above all this, a surer smear of clay on the Pinero foot, and that is the manner in which he deliberately cheats his own theme. That theme, as you know, is the possibility of happiness in marriage between a sensitive man of middle years and a woman with a past. But Pinero never gives the theme a free field and a fair chance. Conscious, perhaps, of his inability to tackle the thesis squarely and work it out to a reasonable philosophical conclusion, he evades the responsibility by so exaggerating and melodramatizing it that he is able shrewdly to persuade his susceptible audiences without convincing them. His Paula Tanqueray is not a woman with merely a past; she is a woman with what may politely be termed a pluperfect. She is a burlesque extravaganza of a woman with a past. She has a record that makes the average guinea pig's look like Peter the Hermit's. She is not beaten and driven to death at length by conventionality in the persons of Ellean and certain of the other characters of the play, but by Pinero, and before she starts. Poor Aubrey's unhappiness is chalked up for him before the first curtain rises. If it hadn't turned out to be Ardale, it might have been the butler.

There is no surer guide to the quality of a man's intelligence and emotions, indeed, than the Pinero drama. The man who still finds himself enchanted and moved by one of Sir Arthur's confections may be quickly put down either as a very young man or as one who is somewhat deficient in the departments of wisdom and experience. For the Pinero drama today is as out-of-date as Stonewall Jackson's socks. It is conceivable that, thirty years ago when this drama was born, there were a few otherwise presumably rational persons who, when they got into a theatre, were profoundly impressed by the Laura Jean Libbey philosophies which Sir Arthur hornswogglingly couched in suave English and caused to be performed by even suaver English actors. But today these philosophies must seem utterly hollow and not a little nonsensical even to such impassionable folk as might have been fetched by them in previous days. I don't wish to posture myself as one of those objectionable duds who, with a lofty condescension, thinks that everybody else in the world has been fooled

212

by something that he himself could see through with one eye shut. Yet surely the majority of Sir Arthur's serious themes have had little or nothing in them that has been above the grade of thesis expounded by Bertha M. Clay, the Duchess and other such favorites of the servant girl of the early nineties. His plays, the most of them, are simply yellow paper-back plots made tony with polysyllables and expensive clothes, with nonchalant allusions to choice cigars, liqueurs, bachelor apartments, yachts, villas in the Riviera and lords and ladies, and with an embroidery of French words and phrases. He is, as ever he has been, an archbishop of the obvious.

§ 8

Drama may not necessarily lie in revolvers, but where there are no revolvers there must be words that flash and gleam and shoot. There are words that are dramatic and words that are not dramatic; there are words that quiver with life and movement as there are others that are supine and sleepy.

§ 9

The Negro is far better fitted naturally for the profession of acting than his white brother. That

the Caucasian more often actually triumphs over
the Ethiopian on the stage is small answer to the
theory, since, so far as that kind of argument goes,
the fact that the Caucasian more often triumphs
over the Ethiopian in the profession of soldiery
similarly does not indicate that the former is by
nature a better fighter than the latter. It simply
indicates, as the more frequent success of the white
actor indicates, that the white man is more susceptible to direction and training, and more indus-
trious, than the black man. The Negro is a born
actor, where the white man achieves acting. He
acts with all the unrestrained and terrible sincerity of which the white actor, save on rare occasions,
is by virtue of his shellac of civilization just a
trifle ashamed. The acting of the Negro is not
acting as John Barrymore knows acting any more
than the singing and dancing of the black Florence
Mills is singing and dancing as Galli-Curci and
Adeline Genée know singing and dancing; it is
something that is just over the borderland of acting
and just this side of the borderland of life and reality. Its essence is ungraspable in print. It is of
the invisible color of Ambrose Bierce's "Damned
Thing" and of the critically elusive quality of certain passages in Strindberg's "Dream Play" or in
Hugo Wolf's "Der Corregidor".

§ 10

With not more than two or three exceptions, it seems to be impossible for the modern French playwright to be sentimental in moderation. Once he starts to feel a bit wistful it is all over with him and his play takes on the appearance of a succession of Hazel Kirkes melting upon the bosoms of as many Lord Traverses, Will Darbyshires and Judith Lovelesses passing cow-eyes, and Little Evas going to heaven. This, peculiarly enough, is true even where the playwright is by nature a humorous and somewhat sardonic fellow: once his foot slips, however slightly, in the direction of sentiment there is no holding him back. Once his heroine breaks from the reins of his humor long enough to look at the hero above the waistline and he is done for. Thus, when the modern French comedy gets out of bed, when the Boulevard des Italiens and the Rue Chaussée d'Antin cease to throw their caps over the mills, as the French put it, and become sentimental *poules mouillées*, the result is disaster. The French playwright can conceive of love above the girdle only as oyster-eyes, trembling under-lips and an off-stage rendition of the "Amour Masqué" waltz. He cannot see the charming humor of pure love;

215

such love ever impresses him as a cross between "La Cathedrale Engloutie" on a harp and "Feuersnot" on a mandolin. Love to him can wear a cap and bells only when the door is locked.

§ 11

Until Eugene O'Neill came along, the American stage knew the sea only as a large piece of canvas painted blue and agitated from underneath by three or four husky members of the Stagehands' Local. The drama that occurred on or in front of the aforesaid canvas consisted chiefly either of a scene on a raft wherein an actress with her hair let down and an actor in a ragged white shirt were supposed to be facing imminent death, said death being duly staved off a minute later by the sudden appearance on the backdrop of two small red and green incandescent lights, representing an approaching, succoring ship, or of a scene in which Abner, the old lighthouse keeper, managed to totter up the winding stairs in time to sound the bell and save the good ship *Mary Louise* from the rocks just before his heart trouble got the better of him. The sailors of the pre-O'Neill days were, similarly, an ingenuous theatrical lot. About the only kinds of sailors that the American drama knew before the estimable Eugene came steaming down the bay were those who showed up at five minutes of eleven off the United States man-o'-war, *San Jacinto,* in the nick of time to save the hero from being eaten by cannibals and those who played opposite fat Irish women comedians in vaudeville sidewalk conversation acts. The sailor of that benighted era was either a hero or a low clown. If the former, he was given principally to periodic loud-mouthed declamations on the superior strength of the American navy to that of England and to scenes wherein he rescued the blonde leading woman from a Chinese opium den just as the electrician turned on the red light to indicate that the dump had been set on fire by the wop villain. And if the sailor was a comedian, he was given to a constant elab-orate hitching up of his pants, to the dancing of a hornpipe, and to the singing of a song called, "I've Got a Girl in Every Port", rendered to the accom-paniment of a number of broad, suggestive winks. O'Neill changed this rich conception of the sea and its people. He made the stage canvas smell less of paint and more of salt; he made the stage sailor smell less of rouge and more of rum and actual-ity. He took the sea and its men out of the old American theatre and gave them life and brought them back into the new American theatre.

§ 12

It is a critical custom in many quarters not to admit that what makes one laugh makes one laugh save the source of laughter be duly endorsed by the Epworth League, the American Legion, the Church White List, the Ku Klux Klan and the New York *Herald-Tribune's* literary supplement. Being, however, constitutionally democratic in the matter of laughter, I usually and disconcertingly have to spoil the reputation for critical nicety that I have laboriously built up over so long a period by confessing that the saloon back-room species of humor not infrequently diverts me in a deplorably gross and welcome manner. I am, alas, the kind of ignoble fellow who laughs at Rabelais, a certain pamphlet of Mark Twain's, the unexpurgated Dean Swift, Walt Whitman's last words, General Grant's bed-time stories, and "Reigen". I am, therefore, doomed to meet Abraham Lincoln in hell.

§ 13

I am wooed by the suspicion that the American commercial theatrical manager opens the manuscript of any play submitted to him in the middle and that if he there finds a wanton word that hasn't been used on the stage before he promptly buys the

play. Thus one comes presently to know exactly
what to expect from the drama sponsored by this
gentleman. Everything moves along prosaically
until about five minutes after ten when suddenly
the air is shattered with a gross and reverberating
mot. Thereafter all settles down peacefully again
and the manager, lighting a fresh Flor de Vedado
Superbissimo Elegancia, calls it an evening and
goes home to bed. The hot word in point generally emanates from one of two scenes, both
equally close to the managerial bosom. The first
of these is one in which a man other than the husband comes casually out of a married woman's
bedroom. The second is one in which a man other
than the husband goes casually into a married
woman's bedroom. A further distinguishing char-
acteristic of the dramaturgy in point is the sex
pourparler. In the second act of the plays put on
by the commercial manager at least ten minutes are
certain to be devoted to a discussion of sex from
what is designated on Broadway as "a new angle."
The aforesaid new angle is generally found to be
slightly more angular than new. For the technic
of these pourparlers consists chiefly either in stat-
ing what everyone has long ago agreed upon in a
very loud and indignant melodramatic tone or in
archly defending a somewhat unpopular view of
the subject by the hokum device of placing all the

customary and popular arguments in the mouth of the villain. In the bulk of the drama, these pourparlers are generally followed by a scene in which someone, after being called a foul name, is either shot or choked. In ordinary life the simple sex act is usually followed by consequences no more dire than those that follow the watching of a parade of the Loyal Order of Moose, but in the glees under discussion it is pretty sure to be followed by a Lincoln J. Carter hullaballoo in which whole families are wiped out by cannon, giant steamships collide with icebergs, cities are swallowed up by earthquakes and murders are committed by the wholesale.

§ 14

Wit, to be effective in the theatre, demands the finished actor, the actor of strictly obedient gesture and feature, of poise and voice humor. Almost any mountebank pulled out of the nearest alley can, given the properly effective clown material, make an audience laugh, but it is the unusual actor, even when given the properly effective wit material, who can make an audience smile.

§ 15

A deep-sea diver goes up in a balloon with only the Spanish army for his companion and meets a green mule named Gladiola who confutes the doctrines of Max Nordau to the dismay of the Greeks. On a clear and stormy night, the deep-sea diver eats a piece of the moon and sings "Mama Goes Where Papa Goes", while the Swedes play pinochle in Akron, Ohio, and the garlic takes an appeal to the higher courts. Yet by virtue of it and despite it, the Brazilians fail to climb Mount Everest and the child is born. After a period of good health and illness, the Italians wade ashore into the sea and are drowned in a sandstorm. The reconciliation of the Poles and Canadians is interrupted by the baking of the mince pies which further causes dissatisfaction among the Iowa intelligentsia, to their sardonic pleasure if not distrust. The rainbow, suddenly shining from the midnight heavens, sets fire to the orphan asylum and Oswald dies.

That, as closely as I am able to figure it out, is the plot of Strindberg's celebrated "The Spook Sonata". The drama is a senseless caricature of the serious theme it purports to deal with. Simply paint the noses of the actors red, put them in wide trousers and change their names from Baron Skansenkorge, Bengtsson and Hummel to Bockheister, Dinkelblatz and Finnegan and, without altering a word of the text, you have an absolutely first-rate burlesque show.

§ 16

Once again each year the theatre hitches up its garters, powders its nose, and saunters forth flirtatiously among the Corinthians and delicatessen dealers. Once again each year the charwomen brush part of the dust off the plush seats, remove the wads of chewing gum from underneath and make ready the house of Thespis for new customers. And once again each year the professional reviewer prepares himself for the old unbeseeming round, occasionally—all too occasionally—illuminated by a shot of purple lightning.

For many years now the reviewer has been deserting dinner at the salad to be on time for some anticipated masterpiece only to arrive on time for the scene in which the tempestuous Zara de Langouste cries out to young Irving Valentino, "This is my hour of madness—but it is the madness of joy! Listen—my villa nestles at the foot of the hill but a short distance from the Hotel de Paris at Monte Carlo as you turn towards the sea. It is overgrown with jasmine and roses. You will find it. Come to me there—tonight. We shall be all alone—you and I and the silent stars!" But yet the reviewer's breast, like the breasts of other men, is human, and in it hope springs eternal. Night in and night out, with the patient stoicism of

an artist's model with the seven years' itch, he seeks
the golden fleece, only too often to find that all that
fleeces is not gold. For one line of beauty like
that in O'Neill's "The Fountain" wherein it is observed of the dreaming Christopher Columbus,
whom the others think mad, that his eyes are full
of golden cities, or for one such line as that of Ros-
tand's Roxanne, "I have loved but one man in my
life—and I have lost him twice", the reviewer
hears a hundred wherein the heroine's eyes are
compared with the Mediterranean or in which the
opera singer beloved of the unsophisticated young
painter is thus vehemently denounced by the latter's friend: "I won't be still! Everyone knows
who Carmen Zuloaga is—but you. Ask Jack Coogan—he knew the Spanish musician chap who
found her singing under hotel windows years ago
in Seville. And Jack knows just when she kicked
him out and went off with that Russian grand duke
and lived with him in Petersburg, until the Prince
de Volailles set her up in Paris! Why, she's notorious all over Europe—she's ruined whole families—run through fortune after fortune—it was
outside *her* door that the young English poet shot
himself—the Emperor borrowed money from the
Rothschilds just to buy her diamonds—the King
of Naples . . . etc." And for one such instance
of cultivated imagination as produces the scene of

the changing lights in Chesterton's "Magic" or the episode of the stubborn symphony gradually finding its harmonic development through love in Fulda's "Friends of Our Youth" or the final satire of the statue scene in Birmingham's "General John Regan", the reviewer finds himself treated like a moron with countless regimented pfuis wherein little crippled girls are miraculously cured through a belief in Swedenborgianism and in which the seducer of the governess turns out to be none other than the son of the clergyman.

But what can one rightfully expect? If the theatre reveals only a few pearls in the round of a year is it any more culpable than the library or the art gallery or the opera stage or the concert hall or one's Château Lafite bootlegger? To expect the theatre to vouchsafe one a steady flow of masterpieces is to expect every new novel to be an "Almayer's Folly", every new offering at the Metropolitan a "Coq d'Or", every new piano masseur a De Pachmann. "The drama", said Lessing, "is, unlike the other arts, often more captivating when it is thoroughly bad than when it is but partly good". (As a matter of fact, Lessing said nothing of the sort. I attribute the remark to him merely to give a greater measure of weight to a statement which, though entirely true, would not be regarded as quite so authentic were it not hitched to the august name of one importantly deceased.) There is, to the reviewer, something fetching about smelly drama. Mr. Ernest Newman might conceivably not be vastly enchanted by the Fadette Lady Orchestra's interpretation of Brahms' "Akademische Festovertüre", nor might Mr. John C. Van Dyke be overpowered by the Attic beauty of Bud Fisher's "Mutt and Jeff", but the dramatic critic who has been in harness for a considerable number of years and who can't still have the time of his life when the hero of an Augustus Thomas play stops in the act of kissing the heroine behind the ear to inform her on the Punic Wars, the later metrical recast in the epic meter of the antecedent Dharmasutras which constitute the Dharmashastras, and the initiative, the referendum and the recall— such a critic is ready for the ax. I speak, of course, not so much of the critic as critic, as mammal with a taste for the low. A bad painting may simply be a bad painting, and so fit only for the gallery of a rich American meat-packer, and a bad piece of music may simply be a bad piece of music, and so fit only for one of the better jazz bands, but a bad play acted by impossible hams is often the joy and delight of kings and emperors. Let a man of unimpeachable taste tell the truth and he will tell you that he has had ten times the pleasure at a No. 3 company's performance of "Uncle Tom's

Cabin" or a No. 4 company's performance of "East Lynne" that he has had at any No. 1 company's performance of the best play that Charles Rann Kennedy ever wrote. I once composed an essay on the charm of bad plays. Such a *concerto grosso,* for example, as "Eve's Leaves" or "Aloma of the South Seas" has thrice the refractory charm of plays fivefold superior. And when a bad play is bitten into by soupy actors—then we have a dish for the gods themselves. Alas, that good form in criticism forbids one's admitting it! For in the admission lies a goodly share of the peculiar pull and peculiar hypnosis of the theatre. It is the good plays that make critics good critics, but it is the bad plays that keep critics young.

§ 17

One of the first requisites of a poetic play is a smooth and harmonious orchestration of the voices of the actors. The finest poetic drama in the world loses its effectiveness in the theatre if the rhythm, timbre and volume of such voices are not carefully regulated. If one-third of the actors have French horns in their throats, and another third czimbaloms, and if the third third read the lines precisely as they would read those of, say, a Fanny Hurst story, the result will obviously be little more than a species of dramatic jazz. A second requisite of such a play is a scenic background that shall melt into the poetry with the curling grace of locomotive smoke. And a third is the achievement of an atmosphere that fitfully covers fancy and reality as with quicksilver, revealing each momentarily yet never revealing each completely—persuading the senses through a voluntary and enchanting confusion.

§ 18

The late war came as a God-send to a certain brand of playwright. Where, before, he had to use a measure of imagination and inventiveness in the manufacture of his plays, he now found that all he had to do to gain a theatrical hearing was to dress up a lot of Pinero or Henry Arthur Jones characters in British uniforms and drown out his weaker dialogue with a terrific walloping of off-stage bass drums. In the early nineties the war play, as Shaw pointed out at the time, was either one in which everybody in both armies turned out to be spies of the other army or in which army commanders were always being superseded at critical moments by their daughters. The recent conflict changed the style. The war play that resulted was, generally speaking, either one that pictured war in terms of Gorki's "Night Refuge" and in which the drama consisted very largely of a liberal employment of the word "guts", or one that pictured it as a kind of Café de la Paix, with all the characters, including the heroine and her pretty school chums, meeting conveniently in a French dugout in the second act and being rather jolly about it all. And, above and below these, we got the play in which François de Pontet-Canet, husband of the loyal Frenchwoman, Madame Germaine de Pontet-Canet, turned out to be none other than Otto von Hofbräu, a German spy; the play in which Jack Terhune and Jim Carruthers, former Yale half-backs, met in the thick of a barrage in the Argonne and, after a half hour's casual conversation, learned that they were both rivals for the hand of Myrtle Weinberg, the Red Cross nurse from Bridgeport; the play in which Fifi Latour, the little French ingénue, discovered that she was about to give birth to a child following an assault upon her by the Kaiser's old valet, Moritz, and, rather than bring a Hun into the world, wrapped the tricolor around her, sang the "Marseillaise" and swallowed bichloride of mercury; the play in which Percy Fothergill, whom all the people at the house-party at Maidenhead dubbed a coward because he would not enlist, turned out in the last act to be a lieutenant-colonel in the British Secret

Service; the play in which the whole German army
was turned back to defeat by a young English cap-
tain's love for a pure woman; the play in which
eight dozen drum-heads were smashed every night
by way of proving how much more ammunition the
Germans had than the Allies; the play in which dying soldiers passed into the Great Beyond talking
wistfully about the flowers in the fields at home
and the beauty of the sunsets behind the old mill;
the play in which a Bataille plot of twenty years
ago was moved from the drawing-room downstairs
into the cellar and played quiveringly in a dim
light, the while the stagehands worked up a huge
sweat pounding a carpet with rattan sticks; the
play in which an erstwhile second-story man and
hophead was miraculously converted into an upright and pious citizen by having lived in a mud-
hole for four years and having come out of it
minus one leg, one eye and both arms and plus a
dose of syphilis, the comic relief of which opus
took the form of Anglo-Saxon grapplings with the
French language; and the play in which the forces
of righteousness were symbolically represented by
an old English squire and the Teutonic marauders
by a strangely bewhiskered glue manufacturer
from the neighboring village who coveted the
squire's virtuous daughter, Gwynne, and also the
old manor house. These plays, one and all, were

either sentimental bushwah or tragic nonsense. They were war in terms of the theatre rather than the theatre in terms of war, which is quite another thing. They portrayed a war in which the commander of the Allied armies was Gerald Du Maurier and the *Hauptoffizier* of the Germans, Rudolph Schildkraut. They were so many pseudo poetic imaginations rhapsodizing musefully over the spiritual *ceintures de chasteté* of Red Cross nurses and the regeneration of sinners by cooties, or, on the other hand, so many pseudo realistic consciences which, confronted by a harsh and unideal theme, translated even the most beautiful flower-bed in terms of its covering of manure. They were, these plays—the most of them—critiques of war written by George Henry Lewes.

§ 19

Too great ambition plays sad havoc with modest, if interesting, talents. Ambition is one of the most dangerous of things. It is safe only for persons of the highest potential mark. Suffered by the average man, it results inevitably in embezzlement, bad Ibsen plays or some other such tragic undoing. The good work in the world is done either by natural-born geniuses, who have small need of ambition, or by lesser talents that are con-

tent to be themselves and are wise enough to keep
their ambitions within self-discerned bounds.
Vaulting ambition had no more share in the birth
of "Moral" than it had in the birth of "Hamlet".
But it has been unchecked ambition, on the other
hand, that has produced such disasters as the blank
verse dramas of Percy Mackaye and the problem
plays of Baron Rothschild. The trouble lies with
the Guy Empeys who aspire to be Wellingtons.

§ 20

The current widespread and eminently commendable impulse among indigenous followers of
the arts to roll the adjective American proudly upon
the tongue is leading to many strange, if understandable, excesses. The wish to build up a thoroughly native art, as opposed, principally, to the
hitherto mongrel Anglo-American thing, is too
often father to the thought of *fait accompli*. In
the Fourth of July excitement, many a squib is
mistaken for a cannon-cracker. This is especially
true of the drama, and we thus presently find ourselves entertained by the promiscuous hailing of
sound Americanism in that department of the arts
when little of the sort is actually visible. Let a
playwright these days so much as show a play in
which no scene is laid at a tea-table and in which

231

the male characters wear coats with ten-inch slits up the back and indulge in a wholesale use of such phrases as the cat's ear-muffs, the turtle's eyebrows and the rhinoceros's spats, and the next morning finds him acclaimed a fellow racy of the soil and of the line of Charley Hoyt, George Ade and George M. Cohan. In the critical rush to enlist under the Stars and Stripes against the Union Jack, everything goes. Any plot shanghaied from the English comedy-drama of twenty-five years ago, laid in Connecticut and with a sufficient number of "aint's" substituted for "aren't I's?" is greeted with millinery in hand and voices lifted in the national anthem. Any ear-dismaying fusillade of old Harrigan and Hart wise-cracks couched in the idiom of present-day Keith vaudeville is ecstatically welcomed as a star against the sky of a new dramatic Bethlehem. And any young man with a derby pulled down over one eye who employs such locutions as "Agitate th' nose-bag, sister!" and who draws his chair up to a table with a red and white cloth on it and eats his soup with his hat on is praised without stint as an authentic contribution to the gallery of American dramatic character portraits.

It is thus that a dozen or more recent plays have been set down as genuine exhibits in Americana when, as a matter of fact, they are rather merely

genuine exhibits in purely theatrical Americana.
They touch the American popular theatre cleverly
at many points, but they touch America and American life at very, very few. They are amusing
American shows, but they are far removed from
authentic American character drawing and authentic American drama. The themes of these
plays are strictly American only in matters of
minor detail; the characters are for the most part
strictly American only in matters of speech; for
the rest the processes of theme, thought, conduct
and action generally are no more integrally American than the theme and characters of, say, a Mos-
enthal peasant drama are generically German, the
theme and characters of Dicento's "Juan José"
generically Spanish, or the theme and characters
of an A. E. W. Mason play generically British.
Such comedies as Hoyt's "A Milk White Flag"
and Ade's "College Widow" are thoroughly American down to the smallest detail; it is inconceivable
that anyone but an American could have thought
of them or written them. Or, for that matter,
could thoroughly understand and appreciate them.
Such comedies, on the other hand, as "Is Zat So?"
and "The Fall Guy", with the speech of certain of
the characters modified and with a change of a few
details, might conceivably have been written by the
Frenchmen, Berr and Guillemand, who wrote

"The Million", or the German, Overweg, who wrote "Piquebube".

The retort here is obviously that, though the themes and the characters of such plays as I have alluded to may not be absolutely and authentically American, save in a highly colored superficial way, the humor that filters from them is. This is to be granted, but only to a degree. For the larger part of the humor of such plays is vastly less true American humor, as the humor, say, of Kin Hubbard, Ring Lardner or Helen Green is true American humor, than the arbitrary and plainly manufactured humor of the American vaudeville stage. This latter species of humor is not so greatly reflective of actual American character and American life as of American theatrical characters and of American life colored to the purposes of the popular amusement platform. It is valid theatrical humor—I often laugh heartily at it with the best and worst of them—but it is surely not humor that is distilled directly from the American soil. It is American humor in the sense and in the degree that Josh Whitcomb, Squire Bartlett and Topsy are American characters.

XV. ATTITUDE TOWARD SEX

§ 1

If I were asked to suggest in a single sentence the essential difference between the Latin and the Anglo-Saxon, I should perhaps put it this way: to the Latin, sex is an *hors d'œuvre*; to the Anglo-Saxon, sex is a barbecue.

§ 2

In the current oppressively ubiquitous cackling of sex, one finds the intelligentsia inclining more and more to the view that sex, far from being the sour-visaged tragedy that it is commonly supposed to be, is really of the essence of pure comedy. While this point of view is, of course, anything but new—having been the established philosophy of all bachelors and Turks over the age of sixteen since the beginning of the Eleventh Century—it seems to me that, for all its major authenticity, it is not without its suspicion of a hole. Sex is a comedy, true enough; it borders, indeed, upon farce; but, like a comedy or a farce, it is played

upon something approximating a theatre stage.
The parties to the performance, the actors, are most
often entirely serious about it, as are the actors of
comedy and farce ever. The humor of sex is enjoyed not by the actors directly concerned in it,
but by the onlookers, the audience. The bride-
groom is not a comedian in his own eyes; he is a
comedian in the eyes of his audience. The bride
herself is wistful and a bit wet of eye; the wheezes
are reserved for the mob around the punchbowl.

Paraphrasing Horace Walpole, sex is a tragedy
to him who feels and a comedy to him who thinks.
In the grip of sex, no man has ever thought. Sex,
to the participant in its theoretical excitements, is
thus ever purely emotional and hence removed, at
least for the time being, from the domain of low
comedy. It may be funny in retrospect, but so too
in retrospect are three-fourths of the tragedies of
the world.

§ 3

Beware the sexlessness of those who talk most of
sex!

§ 4

In the midst of all the somewhat obstreperous
discussion as to whether it is the man or the woman

who is the aggressor in matters of sex, it seems to me to be the most reasonable assumption, based upon a studious and careful investigation of the statistics, that the thing is less a tug-of-war than a tandem. There is no victor; there is no vanquished. The keystone bears engraved upon it the motto, *"Ab hoc et ab hâc"*. As well speak of the aggressor in a piano duet.

§ 5

I can never understand the critic who takes moral objection to sex treated humorously. It is comprehensible that a certain type of mind, so to speak, may find disrelish in certain serious treatments of sex, but my powers of understanding are insufficient to grope with the type of mind that can find offense in any intelligent laughter at sex. It is the outstanding mark of the Anglo-Saxon's philosophical provincialism that he places sex on the farcical index expurgatorius along with his God, his wife, and his pet dog.

XVI. ATTITUDE TOWARD CERTAIN AMERICANOS

§ 1

It is foolish to compare Abraham Lincoln with George Washington. Washington is the symbol of a great achievement; Lincoln merely the symbol of a great hope.

§ 2

With the possible exception of Robert E. Lee, every one of our really great Americans has been by nature and in private life a light-hearted and even waggish man.

§ 3

I never think of Grover Cleveland that I don't think of King Edward VII. They had many qualities in common. Both were charming personalities; both were men who smiled amiably upon the world; both took themselves with the same pleasant measure of unimportance; both were quietly forceful and ever tolerant; both were picturesque;

238

both dictated to others as they would have dictated to themselves; both were free from flapdoodle; both were gentlemen.

§ 4

The death, not long ago, of Richard K. Fox, editor and publisher of the *Police Gazette,* has brought one to ponder afresh on the persistent underestimation of the man that clung to him during his lifetime. Of the editorial generation of Richard Watson Gilder, Henry Mills Alden, Walter Hines Page and Lyman Abbott, Fox—regarded purely as an editor—was the only one of the five to achieve broad international fame, a fame acutely bestowed upon him by foreigners who were shrewd and wise enough to penetrate the prejudice against the man in America and discern his extraordinary talent and capability for the job he had selected as his life's work. Here in America, you will reflect, Fox and his journal were treated mainly as a joke; the two were summarily and idiotically condemned with the designation "barbershop". But the Europeans, the English in particular, were quick to see through the cheap mossback disesteem in which the man and his paper were held and to estimate the fellow in the terms of the peculiar genius that was his. Perhaps not more than two other men—

Dana and Hearst—have exercised so profound an influence as Fox on the practical side of American journalism. This may seem superficially far-fetched, but even a cursory survey of the man's philosophies and practises must convince the skeptic.

Often humorously described as "the paper that everybody read and nobody took", the *Police Gazette* was the first journal in the United States to treat of sports in such wise that the layman could understand what they were about. Fox's editorial plan, since imitated by every journal in America and Europe, changed the entire manner of this kind of reporting. The *Police Gazette*, further, was the first periodical to use a species of tinted paper that made reading easier on the eyes and that, from a commercial point of view, spectacularized the appearance of the paper and made it sell. Consider Fox's imitators in this direction: Bennett and his New York *Telegram*, Pulitzer and the sporting edition of his New York *Evening World*, Hearst and the late editions of his New York *Journal*, to mention only three, and all of these in a single city. There are hundreds of other imitations throughout America; there are two in London; there are two in Paris; there is one in Vienna; there are two in Berlin; there is one in Rome.

Turn to the question of advertising. Fox was, during his life as he remains after his death, the only publisher in America who was not a hypocrite in this direction. He appreciated that the object of printing advertisements was, finally and simply, to make money—and he conducted himself accordingly. "Pay me what I charge and I'll print any dingblasted ad. you give me." That was his intelligent attitude, and that was an attitude that he never changed. The bogus moral pose of his fellow publishers, he had no use for. "Ads.", as he once eloquently put it, "aren't literature; they have nothing to do with the text of my *Gazette;* they are simply extra money in my pocket. Shoot!" The result was that the advertisements in the *Police Gazette* were the most interesting to be found anywhere in America; and the second result was that, being interesting, they made the advertisers almost as rich as Fox himself. There is perhaps not a civilized man in America who does not recall these advertisements, laugh at them as he will. Name another journal of whose advertisements the same thing can be said! And, when all is said and done, advertisements are meant solely to be read and to pay.

Fox was, contrary to opinion in certain benighted quarters, an eminently moral man. Born in Belfast, Ireland, his early training was of a distinctly religious turn, and his career began on the staff of the Ulster *Banner,* a church publication. In all the years that he owned and edited the *Police Gazette,* he never once published, or permitted to be published therein, the photograph of any woman who was not pure. He would print pictures of women in tights—some of them almost nude—but never the picture of one who wasn't, so far as he knew, moral and virtuous. Well, never is perhaps stretching the thing a bit too far, for at one time, during his absence in Europe, a dozen or more pictures of dubious babies got into the *Gazette's* pages and contrived to cast suspicion on Fox's editorial integrity in this quarter. But those in the know never doubted that integrity for a moment, as his prompt dismissal of the guilty sub-editor immediately upon his return from abroad left no further room for suspicion.

The confidant of many famous men—General Ulysses S. Grant, for example, was one of his closest friends, as were Lincoln, Garfield and Grover Cleveland—Fox gained the admiration of everyone who knew him intimately for his clear statement of editorial policy. That policy had but two clauses, and they were as follows:

1. Be interesting.
2. And be damn quick about it.

Fox invented condensed journalism. "Tell your

story in three paragraphs at most", he would order his slaves. "If you can't tell it in three, tell it in two. And if you can't tell it in two, get the hell out of here!"

Fox's influence was felt by the monthly magazines no less than the daily newspapers. The *Century* magazine, for example, today still shows clearly the effect of certain phases of the Fox editorial philosophy, as do to a slightly lesser degree the *Atlantic Monthly*, the *Christian Herald*, and most certainly *The Bookman*.

Fox originated the prize contest, a current favorite circulation-getting device of the dailies and weeklies. He originated the practise of holding various events directly under the auspices of a journal. He originated the motto: "Clean sport for clean people in clean places". Looked on with social disfavor at home, he was the pet of the British aristocracy. Looked on as the editor of a mere low barbershop paper in America, he was regarded on the Continent as the most enterprising, the most audacious and the most thoroughly honest of the American editors of his day.

§ 5

Among the clown shows currently being offered in the Republic for the delectation of all good and true connoisseurs of the bladder and seltzer-siphon, that being staged by Mr. Otto H. Kahn is by all odds the richest in jocosity. Not since Henry Ford almost ruined the vaudeville business with his free peace ship and history-is-bunk performances has the country-side been so entertained. So prismatic are the humors of the exhibition, indeed, that for once in the later history of the nation even the smutty story has given reluctant place to them in smoking-cars, Y. M. C. A.'s and other such quarters where professors of esoteric and ribald mirth are wont to convene.

The Kahn posture, as we know, is the sponsoring of the fine arts. Russian actors, Polish nightingales, French *régisseurs*, Serbian 'cellists, Algerian xylophone players, Iowa little theatres, Bermuda grass weavers, Norwegian dinner-plate tinters, Hawaiian mind-readers, flute players from the Congo Free State, Grand Street Chopins, German acrobats, Spanish glass-blowers, Cincinnati minnesingers, Canary Island novelists, Irish classical dancers, Mexican stereopticon lecturers, Scotch moving picture directors, Greek cuspidor designers—all are wholesalely embraced in the Kahn entrepreneurship. Does it come to the Kahn eardrum that in Bpolpz, Hungary, there is a blonde *fräulein* who can reach high C without bursting more than two

244

corset strings, then does Kahn—after 316 newspaper interviews in which his name is casually
mentioned 4,316 times—bring her to these shores
where, after the ship news reporters have been sent
down to persuade her casually to mention Mr.
Kahn's name a few more times, she is permitted to
regale the natives with her art until such a period
as she is no longer good copy for the interviewers
and hence of no service to Mr. Kahn in getting his
name into the papers. Or does a young boy with
an aptitude for playing Bach on the oboe show up
in Wzyczk, Poland, then does Kahn similarly—
after a large banquet to the Sunday supplement
editors and writers—bring him westward that we
Americans may not be allowed to starve for the
great art of the Continent. It is roughly estimated
that, up to the moment, our friend has imported
3,216 actors, 974 singers, 4,639 musicians, 2,817
ballet dancers, 816 directors of different sorts,
1,256 painters, 832 sculptors, 2,642 poets, and
168,358 newspaper interviews. Every time a far-
off mother smiles her first smile at a baby whom
God has sent into the world to gladden it in coming
years with beautiful art, our friend orders another
bottle of paste for his own scrapbook. And every
time, after years of hardship and misery, a man
or a woman comes at length into the power of the

art that he or she has faithfully, bravely and desperately striven for, he renews his order for clippings with Romeike.

The spectacle, for all its ironic humor, is, however, just a bit touched with sadness. Art is a noble and dignified and very lovely thing: one of the few noble and dignified and very lovely things that we have left to us these days in this hate-torn, money-lustful, party-rent world. To see it thus made mock of at the hands of vainglory and attitudinizing is hurtful to many of us. If Kahn were to go about his self-imposed task of sponsorship quietly, simply, and just a little humbly, he might do great good where he now does but harm. For one cannot inspire the peoples of a country if first they have been made to snicker contemptuously. There is room in America for a great patron of the arts; but there is not room for one who uses the arts in the manner that Barnum used the bearded lady and that a moving-picture actress uses her series of husbands.

§ 6

Harriet Beecher Stowe was the lady Upton Sinclair of her day. She wished, in her stupendous vanity, to be a tracker-down, a scooter after fugitives, an instrument of vengeance, which is to say,

justice. Had she lived in 1907, she would have
written Thomas W. Lawson's books. Had she
lived in 1912, she would have written "My Little
Sister" and the other white-slavery brochures.
Had she lived in 1915, she would have written
Cleveland Moffett's "Invasion of America". Were
she alive today, she'd be bawling for the Blue
Laws.

§ 7

Poor old Dr. Frank Crane has been the goat for
so long that one hesitates to drag him again from
his contentful licking of philosophical tomato cans
out onto the slapstick platform, but the temptation
in this instance proves stronger than the sympathy.
I therefore present the good Doctor's latest schnitz'l
of wisdom. "Criticism", observes the good Doctor, "is the easiest thing in the world. It does not
take a thimbleful of brains to find fault and the
biggest numskull in the world can find fault with
the greatest man in the world. We flatter ourselves that criticism is a sign of superior intelligence. It is not. It is usually a sign of bad manners, of lack of self-restraint, and of an entire ignorance of psychology."

Brief illustrative lists of numskulls: Renan,
Huxley, Spencer, Goethe, Nietzsche, Carlyle, Dar-

247

win, Schlegel, Kant, Voltaire, Molière, Dryden, Lessing, Poe, Shaw, Brandes, Croce. . . .

§ 8

Nothing could be more typically American than the extravagant hymns lifted not long ago by the newspapers upon the demise of John Wanamaker. Wanamaker was an affable fellow, an estimable citizen and an exceptionally able business man—that, in simple, was his record. But the newspapers, doubtless with a shrewd eye to the effect their goose-grease would have upon such other still living fellow merchants and big advertisers as Straus, Saks, Gimbel and the others, unloaded eulogies upon him that would have befitted a Napoleon, Bismarck and Jesus Christ in combination. A canny trick! The other big merchants, as the big merchants themselves acutely appreciated, would die some day too—and meanwhile it would be well for them to keep in the good graces of the newspapers with heavy advertising, as Wanamaker had done.

I have read some twenty or thirty obituaries of Wanamaker. Each and all, they are almost grotesquely out of key with a just and sensible appraisal of the man, his life, and his work in the world. If the vastly more important Alexis Carrel, say, were to die tomorrow, would these newspapers, purged of selfish motives, treat him in the same way? A glance at a sample of the Wanamaker drool, culled from one of the New York dailies, gives a sufficiently sweet idea of the bosh of the business. I quote:

"He dreamed dreams. He had vision, foresight, around-sight, seeing ahead of his day, his generation, even seeing through brick walls by seeing around them into people's homes, into people's hearts. He would rise to the stars. . . . He dared to *do*. He was free—and he made others free. He had the 'third eye'; his powers of observation were almost uncanny; he seemed to have eyes all over him; nothing escaped him. He saw service and usefulness wherever he looked—in a barren field, in a pile of rubbish, in a blank wall. He saw through the wall to the beauty and utility on the other side. This gift was undoubtedly the spiritual eye—the third eye—that only genius has! He was always searching for the good in others, ignoring or correcting their faults. He accepted no limitations. When people were saying 'It can't be done', he was doing it. He was not bound by conventions nor limitations nor conditions—he overcame them. His mind grasped the big things of life. He always did the unexpected. So much

249

was this true that some of his associates used to figure on the very opposite of what John Wanamaker was expected to do—and this opposite would be the best guess. He deliberately planned originality. One seemed to breathe his hospitality in with the air. In reality it was *Wanamaker atmosphere!* John Wanamaker was a youth at eighty. With little schooling, he educated himself *as few men have been educated.* He was seldom without a book in his hand. He kept himself open continually to the flow of the creative spirit through him. He was always breaking records. Above even most great men he knew and practised the law of life: Give and ye shall receive. He gave his all to the world. And he received almost all the world has to give. Not empty honors. Not office. Not great pecuniary reward. But the good-will of the people. . . . He ennobled service. *He made business a profession equal to any other profession.* Acknowledging all his long life the source of his power as coming from God, he revered and worshiped everything that comes from God".

If John Wanamaker, a man of good hard, cold sense, could read this nonsense, he undoubtedly would loosen a top pant-button, open the window for more air, and laugh himself red in the face.

§ 9

Another year has gone since they laid Jim Huneker in his grave. Another year has gone since they laid in the same grave the most dazzling conversation that America has known.

XVII. ATTITUDE TOWARD VICE, VIRTUE AND CENSORSHIP

§ 1

When ultimately they get down the big white and black ledgers on the Day of Judgment and begin checking up the accounts of mortal man, I have a feeling that it will be the Devil and not St. Peter who will get the Pulitzer prize. Virtue is going to have a tough job proving its realistic superiority to sin. For every person who was made happy on earth by virtue, the Devil will have no difficulty in calling off the names of twenty who were made thrice as happy by moral obliquity. When St. Peter calls off the name of some sweet-faced *religieuse* who gave her life and all her world to God, the Devil will let out a horse-laugh and name the dozen dazzling mistresses to the great kings of France. When St. Peter calls off the name of some pious brother who slaved for the spiritual welfare of his people, the Devil will take another chew of tobacco and name nine-tenths of the poets who have sung the music of the world since first the world began. And when both are finished there will be drawn up, on the one side and on the other, two lines. Behind St. Peter there will be a line of .pale, beautiful, sad men and women, their eyes ennobled with tears, their tired feet made ready to climb the reward of holy and golden stairs. Behind the Devil there will be a longer line, a line of women with necklaces of pearls and rubies and of men with brilliant red noses, their faces tired from laughter but laughing still in the richness of their memories, waiting for the Pullman to hell.

§ 2

Let any professional censor, when he starts out to clap the lid on any book or play or picture or piece of sculpture on the ground that it may be subversive of the morals of the young of the species, look back upon his own youngsterhood. Let him ask himself if in that period of his life he, like all other youngsters, didn't have a few dirty ideas and didn't commit a few moral misdemeanors. And let his answer to himself—to be kept his own secret property—be absolutely honest. This done, let him then ask himself what share any book or play or picture or piece of sculpture had in the matter.

253

§ 3

In a general way, it may be said that artist and censor differ in this wise: that the first is a decent mind in an indecent body and that the second is an indecent mind in a decent body.

§ 4

Despite the wails that are still lifted whenever censorship is mentioned, it should be clear to a man with cinders in both eyes that never before in the history of American literature and drama have things been so happily free from interference by professional indignantos as they are at the present time. Books are published today that so little as three years ago would have been raided before the ink was dry, and plays are shown that, no less than two years back, play juries or no play juries, would have brought down a veritable hurricane of gendarmes. Only the movies are still subjected to a rigorous censorship, and they should be. Being for the most part composed of unspeakable garbage, it matters not in the least the one way or the other to any intelligent person what is done to them. The more that is cut out of them, says he, the better.

254

And what has brought this pleasant state of affairs about? The answer is ready to hand. That answer is ridicule. When a Methodist gets home after an elegant and grandiose promenade up the boulevard and finds that, in the early stages of the promenade, someone has pinned to his tail a placard reading "Please kick me!", his grand tour of the following day is ever certain to be one of humbler mien. The professional censors have thus been made to seem comparative jackasses in their own eyes, and day by day they are being made to seem more so to themselves. They are beginning to have difficulty in convincing others of their dignity and importance. They have asked for cheers, and they have got the raspberry. To be a censor today, accordingly, a man must be not only an idiot; he must be also a man courageous enough in his imbecility to endure the low guffaws of his next-door neighbors. And that is a job too hard to bear for such idiots as censorship is generally made of.

§ 5

The Puritan looks on breakfast as the beginning of a new day. The anti-Puritan looks on breakfast as the end of the day before.

255

§ 6

Of all the days in the year, there is at least one regarding which the moralists need have no concern. That day is the thirtieth of December. A study of statistics for the last twenty-two years shows that on this particular day the morals of the community are higher than on any other day of the calendar: there are fewer crimes, fewer arrests, fewer wife-beatings, fewer bawdy divertissements, and fewer cases of alcoholism. It is on this day that the Americano takes a rest from sin in preparation for the grand and glorious New Year's Eve debauch due the following night. It is on this day, of all days, that he holds himself in check and stores up energy for the imminent exploration of the vices, excitements and tipples of Sodom, Gomorrah, Milwaukee and points West.

It is said that in the entire city of New York not more than fifteen cocktails are consumed on the thirtieth of December. Bartenders have always regarded the day as a holiday to be spent at home with their wives and children. Taxicabs go into their garages at midnight; the streets are deserted a few minutes later; there is no call for them. Ladies of joy retire at quarter of nine for their annual beauty sleep. The cabarets and honkatonks write down losses of thousands of dollars, and the

Chinatown sight-seeing buses, those migratory
yoshiwara, are left empty at the street corners.
The most brilliant and dazzling red nose gets back
a tittle of its old, natural color, and the old rheu-
matic pain in the left leg lets up a trifle. There
are no arguments, no fist fights; and the bellhops
in the clubs take a snooze on the divans in the deserted libraries and esoteric upstairs bib-rooms.
The air is silent; the world waits. Twenty-four
hours of moral grace before hell breaks loose
again.

§ 7

I unearthed it in a little second-hand book shop
down in Astor Place. It is a resplendent tome published by Funk and Wagnalls in 1883; its piquant
title is "Traps For the Young"; and its author is
no less a celebrity than that immortal Fanny Hill-
billy, the late Mons. Anthony Comstock, in his
time secretary and chief special agent of the New
York Society for the Suppression of Vice. The
book is, in the language of the Society for the
Preservation of the Purity of the English Language,
a fruit. And it affords, after the lapse of these
forty-odd years, a not altogether unhumorous picture of the genesis of the anti-vice wave that has
since swept across the American scene and of the

nature of the droll little acorns from which the more recent towering prune trees have flourished.

The frontispiece to the book is in the tasty early Al Woods manner, bears the legend "The Modern News Stand and Its Results", and is divided into five sections. In the centre, we behold a number of youngsters gathered around a street newsstand. The dire consequences of this act are pictured to the right and left. One cut shows one of the tots holding up an adult pedestrian with a revolver and shouting, "Your money or your life!" Another shows several of the youngsters smoking pipes and cigars. A third depicts a little boy about to stab another little boy. And the fourth shows a couple of bairns enjoying themselves by setting fire to a house. All of which is, you will observe, a direct result of having stood in front of a street newsstand.

But let us proceed to the cookie itself. It appears from the table of contents that life in those days was—and by implication is still—just one damn trap after another. I quote them: Chapter I., Household Traps; Chapter II., More Household Traps and Newspaper Traps; Chapter III., Novel and Story Paper Traps; Chapter IV., Advertisement Traps; Chapter V., Gambling Traps; Chapter VI., Poke-a-moke or Policy Traps; Chapter VII., Pool Traps; Chapter VIII., Death-traps

ATTITUDE TOWARD VICE, VIRTUE, CENSORSHIP
by Mail; Chapter IX., Quack Traps; Chapter X.,
Free Love Traps; Chapter XI., Artistic and Classical Traps; Chapter XII., Infidel Traps, Liberal
Traps, etc.; Chapter XIII., More Liberal Traps;
Chapter XIV., Appendix of General Traps. All
these traps, like the bed-time stories of today, it
develops, were for little boys and girls. "After
more than eleven years' experience contending for
the moral purity of the children of the land", begins the solicitous author, "I have one clear conviction, *viz.:* (the book is chock full of *vizes*) *that
Satan lays the snare, and children are his victims.*
There is a great variety of traps used by mankind.
For instance, the fox trap, the box trap, the rabbit
trap, the squirrel trap, the partridge trap, the
bear trap, the mink trap, the rat trap and the mouse
trap. Satan adopts similar devices to capture our
youth!" Satan's murderous traps for the unwary
American child are then attacked head on by the
good Comstock. It would seem that the love story
is one of the most dangerous of all Satan's traps
for the little ones. "It captivates fancy and per-
verts the taste of the child", says Comstock. "It
defrauds the future man and woman by enslaving
the young imagination. Even in the sanctuary
during the solemn hours of worship on the Sabbath
day, it makes the day-dreamer wander away in
thought". Born at about the time Mr. Comstock's

book was published, I can verify his asseverations by confessing that my own long criminal record was directly due to my having read as a small boy the love stories of Jane Austen.

Turning to page 11 of the book, I encounter this lovely sliver of literary criticism: "In novel reading, the tendency is from the higher to the lower rather than from the lower to the higher. . . . Some have questioned whether persons reading such authors as Mrs. Southworth and Alexander Dumas advance in time to George Eliot *and Sir Walter Scott.*" "Light literature, then," concludes St. Anthony, "is a devil-trap to captivate the child . . . and rob the future ages of the high order of men and women". As samples of particularly dangerous stories he specifies those in which (*1*) beautiful girls seek to captivate men they love, (*2*) in which beautiful girls are forced to marry scoundrels to save their benefactors, (*3*) in which women die in New York and come to life in Italy, (*4*) in which Indians commit massacres, (*5*) in which babes are stolen and substituted for other babes (*e. g.,* the vicious and demoralizing "Pinafore"), (*6*) in which heartless wretches marry young ladies of "princely beauty", (*7*) in which heartless wretches marry haughty rich young women; and (*8*) in which "men on the way from their second wedding ceremonies pass their first

260

wives who fall dead lisping their names", and in which—I quote from Prof. Comstock's book—"the heartless villain is then led to his new and elegant home and is made to say: 'Not within sight of my window could I bear the narrow mound; not within sound of the voice of my haughty titled bride should she lie. So I carried her away . . . still in her bridal gown of white, to rest forever!'" Such stories, proclaims the author, "do more to debase the young than an endowed chair in every college in the land will or can do to ennoble them!" "Only recently", then indignantly climaxes Dr. Comstock, "I purchased a book the web of whose story consisted of . . . a street fight, wine drinking, *smoking cigars,* et cetera!" Such vile fables, he states, "destroy domestic peace, desolate homes, and make foul-mouthed bullies, cheats, vagabonds, thieves, desperadoes, and libertines!"

As a result of reading stories of this kind, Le Comstock points to three specific cases:

"Last April" (he writes) "a lad fifteen years of age was arrested after three attempts to wreck a train just beyond Saratoga. Pleasant thought for the traveler, that we are safe from the armed brigands of Italy and the outlaws of the plains, but in imminent danger from schoolboys crazed by the accursed story papers!"

"A short time ago"—this is Case 2—"a lad ran

away from home. He had played truant from school, and had been punished by his parents. This was too much for him! No boy in a ten-cent story would stand that! He joined a band of youthful robbers who had a rendezvous in an old unoccupied house. He was initiated at night, with ceremonies and a solemn oath to secrecy, *after which a banquet was served!*"

Another lad perhaps not more than seven years old—this is Exhibit C, and a heart-rending one, as you will presently perceive—read stories and also ran away from home. This is what Comstock says happened to him as a result of reading stories. I quote literally: "He went to New Orleans, there had an attack of fever, and came very near dying among strangers. After that he went to Galveston, where he broke his arm. Then he stole a ride to Houston on a freight train, and there was pushed off the train, breaking two ribs. After recovering he was wounded by a pistol shot, and then got into a fight and was beaten almost to death. After this, to get a living he had to sell papers, black boots, work in a livery stable, cut heavy timbers, and herd cattle on the plains in the far West".

Some kid!

There are at least a dozen other similarly harrowing and piteous stories that show with equal force, clarity and conviction the pernicious influence of literature upon the young.

Turning to lotteries—one of the most iniquitous of Satan's traps for our babies—Mr. Comstock says, "Tickets are placed on sale in some of the lowest dens in our large cities. In these places I have repeatedly seen children standing with trembling forms waiting their turn".

Traps for tots, No. 602 G: "Certain manufacturers of cigarettes, in order to fix more forcibly a taste and habit and fasten upon the youthful smoker the uncontrolable practice of smoking, *put opium in their cigarettes.* It seems as if Satan hems in our youth in all directions".

"In stories about detectives", proceeds the author, sounding a warning against such cigarette propaganda literature, "you will find at all conferences choicest wines and liquors are brought out, while they lay back in their chairs, feet upon the mantel (Note: India rubber detectives, evidently) or table, while the blue smoke curls above their heads as it is puffed out of their mouths in fantastic forms. *These are not imaginary evils!*"

Trap for bambinoes, No. 603 H: "But lest children shall be let off too easy, and to block up more effectually every avenue of escape, we have another devil-trap for even the little wee ones. These traps may be discovered in confectionery stores which keep open on Sunday. Any person who has observed these matters must have been struck with the numbers of little ones who throng into candy stores *before* and *while going* to Sunday-school. It is when their faces are turned away from home and its hallowed influences, toward the sacred precincts of God's house to be trained up in wisdom and grace, that the Evil One overtakes them and makes a bid for them. Tempted by the delicious flavors so sweet to the taste, dishonesty is encouraged and swiftly follows".

Most dastardly of all Satan's traps for the papooses, No. 604 K, it appears, is billiard pool. "Pool", writes Mr. Comstock, who apparently was not an observant pool player, "is a game played on a billiard table". "Children become so infatuated with it", he says, "that speedy ruin overtakes them". As an unanswerable argument against all pool playing, Mr. Comstock states that on September 22, 1882, Charles H. Warren shot Patrick Dwyer over a game of pool in a saloon at No. 108 Bowery. It will be seen from this, he concludes, that "pool gambling is only another subtle scheme of Satan to ensnare our youth".

Trap for innocents, No. 716 A, is "The defilement of the young by handkerchief and glove flirtation cards, by which means the schoolgirl is taught how to respond to a code of signals printed on little cards". I look back with considerable alarm at what might have happened to me at the hands of the six-year-old hussy who, when I was the same age, used to drop her handkerchief in kindergarten as a foul signal to me to give her a go at my cinnamon lollipop.

I haven't room for Traps from No. 717 A to No. 2,615 W. So I shall wind up the show with selections from Mr. Comstock's quoted diatribe against the poor Turks and what free love has done to them:

"The great majority of modern Turks are of an effeminate type. . . . After the age of forty in the women, there remains no trace of the physical strength often seen in English women of sixty-five or even seventy. . . . Another immediate result is the mental imbecility of multitudes of the Ottoman Turks; many of even the young men have the vacant look which borders close on the idiotic state. . . . The royal family itself has been devoid of mental capacity. . . ."

And yet there were some folks in those days who read the books of Petroleum V. Nasby and Bill Nye!

§ 8

One of the most dubious phrases in the English language is that which concerns "the earning of an honest living". The earning of this honest living, as it is called, often wears sardonic cardboard ears and an ornate putty nose. Among the men who earn this honest living, as the Americano regards it, are, for example, salesmen of cachoo powder, which, placed on the arm of grandma's chair, makes her sneeze her head off, five cent smell-bombs, loaded cigars, marked decks of cards, oil stocks, correspondence courses that guarantee to teach women how to become Irene Castles in five lessons and men how to become Thomas Nasts in four, horoscopes, rejuvenators that will make octogenarians feel like Jackie Coogan, three dollar and a half diamonds, nose-straighteners that are put on at bedtime and convert a proboscis that resembles half a doughnut into a retroussé snout by Saturday night, and a thousand other such things. All of these entrepreneurs are safe from the hoosegow, all are more or less respected members of their particular communities. Men who do not earn their living honestly, as the Americano looks on it, and who are therefore not safe from the bastille, are, on the other hand, those, for example, who sell information to the destitute and agonized mother of ten children how to keep from giving birth to an eleventh, who publish fine pieces of literature that are regarded as obscene

266

ATTITUDE TOWARD VICE, VIRTUE, CENSORSHIP

by those small boys who never get over playing
with their *Schmutzigkeit*, to wit, the professional
censors and moralists, and who sell a glass of
blackberry brandy to a man half-crazy with a terrible stomach-ache.

XVIII. ATTITUDE TOWARD LOVE AND MARRIAGE

§ 1

Love is always a tragedy for the woman. That tragedy she never succeeds entirely in escaping. It is sometimes the tragedy of a broken heart, sometimes the greater tragedy of fulfilment. A broken heart is a monument to a love that will never die; fulfilment is a monument to a love that is already on its death-bed.

§ 2

Of the two loves—that which is felt deeply and that which is simulated—the second becomes the stronger with the passing of time. A woman, for example, forgets the grand passion of her life in the paraphrased and substitute love that has brought her a husband, a home and, with the flood of the years, peace and ease and a remote tranquility.

§ 3

Perhaps the happiest time in the average hans-doodle's life is three weeks before his marriage.

268

It is then that the lady of his knightly yen is just far enough from his reach to enravish and englamor him and yet not near enough to give him that moment of dubiety and pause that comes, in such cases, to even the humblest of God's boobs. The altar is still remote enough to gain enchantment from the loan of distance and not close enough to frighten him. The hansdoodle thus stands momentarily in that most beautiful of all lands, the no-man's land of romantic love. But as the three weeks draw nearer and nearer to the amorous electric chair, his happiness grows correspondingly less and less. For the hansdoodle, no less than the rest of us professors, gradually begins to be besieged by doubts, soever small, that he actually wants what he wants when he wants it. Three weeks ago, he gave up nothing—nothing of freedom, nothing of irresponsibility, nothing of tzigane fancy. But now, at the altar, he sees in a flash what he is leaving behind him—all those things that he has convinced himself he no longer cares for but which yet, as he climbs the church steps, begin to seem never so slightly desirable. His pulse beats with happiness, but his mind ticks with a faint homesickness for the security of the day before, and the day before that, and the days and days before them. And then the honeymoon. And then the hundred and one inevitable little nuisances and concerns that take just a bit of the edge off an erstwhile inviolate romantic dream. And then the days ahead. Often happy, these days, doubtless, but days that miss something—that all important and forever vanished something—of those glad and trembling days three weeks before his anticipation, his illusion and his love were duly checked and labeled.

§ 4

To say that nine-tenths of marriages are unhappy is doubtless untrue. But, looking about me, I venture, and not without a reasonable amount of confidence, the opinion that the marriages that are happy are chiefly those in the period of the twenties and those of the early fifties and beyond. Marriage in these groups of years is apparently pleasant and agreeable to the parties concerned; during these spaces of time there seems to be little or no disagreement or unhappiness. But marriage during the period of the thirties and forties is apparently fraught with trials and tribulations. The couple that hangs together in perfect accord during its thirties and forties is as rare as the ducatoon of Priuli.

270

§ 5

A man's wife is his compromise with the illusion of his first sweetheart.

§ 6

It is a popular belief, largely cultivated by men themselves, that man is a rooster who would achieve grand delight and satisfaction if, like his Turkish brother, he were permitted to have a harem. While it is perhaps true that here and there one might find a barber, or a jewelry drummer or a movie actor who would actually enjoy such an arrangement, it is far from true that the average man would relish it in the slightest. The average man would care for a plurality of women no more than he cares for a plurality of pairs of patent leather shoes. His taste is pretty uniformly for one woman, one toothbrush, one flag. That taste may undergo a change, of course; it often does. But he would have no more use for six or seven wives—spiritually, emotionally or physically—than he would have for six or seven back collar buttons. To argue that, because of his biological nature, he would have use for a harem is to argue that, because of his biological nature, he would have use for a dozen bathrooms.

271

§ 7

Marriage is the reward that women graciously withhold from the men they have truly loved.

§ 8

A close student of matrimony of many years' standing, it seems to me that the average male candidate for the honor is as greatly in need of professional advice as any other ailing man and that, neglecting to seek this advice, he lays himself open to quite unnecessary risks and hazards. When a man plans to get married—and many a man plans to enter the matrimonial state, whether by instinct, hereditary impulses, tradition, or in the interests of what he believes to be his future well-being and happiness, long before he has picked out the woman who is to be his wife—when, as I say, such a man plans to engage nuptial bliss he seldom if ever seriously considers what type of woman would be the best and safest, and not only the best and safest but the most beneficent, to take unto his bosom. Love, beauty, character, position—such things he meditates upon, but he gives no thought to subjects of much bulkier importance and, giving them no thought, often learns of them, much to his sorrow, when it is too late.

ATTITUDE TOWARD LOVE AND MARRIAGE

It is my belief, and I pass on the suggestion to young men contemplating holy wedlock, that an orphan is perhaps of all women the one best fitted to be a desirable wife. The fact that she is an orphan automatically gets rid of the father-in-law and mother-in-law nuisance. She is alone in the world and grateful to the man who marries her. Having no one who is very close to her, her husband will seem closer to her than he would to a wife whose parents, or at least one of whose parents, were still living. Furthermore, the orphan is always the more tractable, wistful and tender woman. She has known sorrow, and sorrow, as the old saw wisely hath it, maketh a woman beautiful in the heart. But if the young man open to the lures and splendors of matrimony does not happen to love an orphan, but loves instead, shall we say, a widow, what advice then? My advice then--and I may be forgiven for observing that it is grounded upon a study of the problem ranging over a period of thirty-five years—my advice is to marry only a widow whose first husband either beat her or who died disgracefully, as by having been hanged or being shot in a bawdy house or getting ptomaine poisoning from a free-lunch kippered herring. If the widow's first husband is *in absentia* for other reasons or by virtue of a dignified demise, she will begin to think of

him and brag about him a few years after her
second marriage, and that marriage will then
quickly begin heading for the rocks. Only the
widow who hates the memory of Spouse I can make
a happy mate for Candidate II. But, yet again,
if it is neither orphan nor widow that our ambi-
tious young man has his passion set upon, what
then? Well, let us assume that the creature of
our young friend's choice is a pea-chick possessed
of considerable wealth, and who is neither orphan
nor widow. In this event my long years of investigation and research impel me to discharge the
advice that our young friend consider marrying
such a petitioner only if he himself be a very poor
man. The marriage of a rich young woman and
a very poor young man is revealed by the statistics
to be generally a happy one, and for a simple reason, whereas the marriage of a rich young woman
and a rich young man all too often turns out badly.
The rich young man who marries a rich young
woman gains nothing from the marriage, or at best
little, in comparison with the poor young man.
The latter's improved position and comfort oper-
ate to make his wife more desirable in his eyes
and a marriage that might otherwise end in disaster is thus often perpetuated and made happy
until death. There have been cases where a rich
woman has kicked her poor husband out of the

house, but so far as I know there has never been a case where a poor husband has kicked his rich wife out of the house.

I further always urge my protégés to marry pretty women. The best of women get homely all too soon, and it is well to have a pretty wife at least for a beginning. A pretty wife for five or six years is something: it makes, in memory and retrospect, romantic amends for the damaged wife one must live with in the many years that loom ahead of and beyond these first five or six years. The additional advantage of marrying a pretty girl as opposed to a homely one is obvious. The pretty girl will take out all her spoiled nature, whims and outside flirtations on her husband at the very outset, and thus get them over with. After a few years, when she loses her looks, she will settle down and behave herself, and give her husband no trouble. The homely girl, to the contrary, having no looks to fall back on or bother about, will begin by being twice as sweet and attentive to her husband as the pretty girl, but will end up by taking revenge on him for all the early outside flirtations that she never could enter into and enjoy and that, unlike in the instance of the pretty girl, thus never provided her with an opportunity to let off the steam of her vanity.

I need not pursue the subject farther, at least

today. If I have so much as suggested that there is some truth in my prefatory assumptions, I shall be content. I desire merely to add, in conclusion, that all the young men who have thus far followed my advice are happy husbands and fathers. Their wives never fail to remember me, with excellent cigars, at the Yuletide.

§ 9

Women begin to think of marriage on the day that they first feel old; men on the day that they first think old. The thought of marriage enters a woman's head when the past and all its gay and crowded uncertainties seem about to slip from hands that may no longer grasp and toy with them; the thought of marriage enters a man's head when the future and all its grim and lonely uncertainties seem about to slip from hands that, save they grasp them now, may never have the opportunity to convert them into peace and comfort and certainty. No woman, in the highest moment of her happiness, thinks of marriage. She begins to think of it in her moments of misgiving, self-doubt and misery. Marriage, with her, is generally a craft that backs quickly out to sea from a shaky and partly condemned dock.

§ 10

Love is the democrat of the emotions; hatred the aristocrat.

§ 11

The institution known to civilized society as the husband vouchsafes to the student-connoisseur of the *comédie humaine* a source of profitless but none the less diverting speculation. Why, for example, should this husband, as he is called, in nine cases out of ten be to the woman whom he has taken unto his bosom a comic figure, one to snicker at silently or to razz more or less openly after the second cocktail has got in its fine Italian vermouth hand? This husband's wife is certainly not a comic figure, as he himself is, nor does he even for an instant so regard her, yet there he stands a target for her internal derisions and for the derisions, perhaps more charitable, of persons removed from his own hearth and home. My pondering of the problem in behalf of this unfortunate fellow creature has brought me to various conclusions, some of which I have the honor here to divulge.

Courtship, as everyone, including the parties thereto, knows, is a show, a spectacle. This show devolves largely upon the man, for, while it is not a new business for the woman—since woman is in the show business from the cradle to the grave —it is a comparatively new business for the man. Finding himself in love, as the phrase is, he synchronously finds it necessary for himself to take on the emotional and mental attributes of an actor, and to conduct himself much after the manner of a mime cast for the leading rôle in a romantic drama. In the degree that he succeeds in this is he successful in impressing, captivating and winning the heart and hand of his lady love. For it is customarily this actorial projection of her suitor that the lady becomes enamored of and, enveloped in the purple haze it gives out, capitulates to. But no man not an actor by profession can keep up, or feels like keeping up, the performance once the show is over. Some husbands, true enough, go bravely on with the grease-paint comportment and proscenium behavior for a variable number of years after the wedding bells have rung, but soon or late they lapse back into the *status quo*, into the plain, unromantic fellows they were before the divine passion, as the phrase also is, beset them. The moment the husband thus goes back to normal, that moment does his wife, with the wisdom of safely married women ever, translate her disillusion, usually calmly anticipated, into comfortable comedy. The lover's mask is off and he is revealed as simply a poor clown who is often still lovable but who, for all that, is yet a poor clown: a human being who is half a Rudolph Rassendyl with a two-day's growth of beard and half a neatly shaved meal-ticket.

But while this process of actorial disintegration is going on in the husband, the actorial talents of the wife increase in proportionate ratio. As if realizing that the two of them are cast for a single rôle in the tragi-comedy of the matrimonial relation and that one of them has, so to speak, forgotten his lines, the wife appreciates that it is her duty to carry on the show alone, single-handed. In this, her long and natural training in romantic artifice stands her in good stead. And thus, while her husband appears to her as a once handsome cuspidor from which all the enamel has been chipped, she continues to appear to the old spittoon a relatively theatrical and effective figure. The average husband is approximately as romantic to his wife as a cow. But despite all the published cynicism to the contrary, the average wife, I fully believe, is a more or less romantic figure to her husband. By romantic I do not, obviously, necessarily mean the creature of starshine and wild white clover that she was before, during and directly after the woo period, but romantic as a

279

man's close possessions remain ever romantic in
his eyes, as the scrapbook of his university days,
or his old meerschaum pipe, or his dog. It is for
the reason that everyone outside of himself is privy
to him that the husband is viewed more or less
generally as the pitiable figure in an extravaganza:
an actor who once played the leading rôle in romantic "Old Heidelberg" condemned now by
ironic nature and by homely fate to the permanent
rôle of butler in a hinterland stock company.

§ 12

A man sometimes enters upon a new love affair only to protect himself from the irritatingly
enduring sentiment of the previous one.

§ 13

In the many learned and eloquent treatises on
divorce that have appeared in the various public
prints, it seems to me that I and my colleagues in
secular philosophy have at times laid too much
stress on important things and too little on trivial.
The adjectives are used, of course, in their generally accepted sense; hence there is no paradox.
What I mean to say, specifically, is this: that the
causes of divorce are doubtless infinitely more insignificant, as such things go, than the majority

of investigators and examiners believe. The real causes, that is. The reasons that appear in court are generally as far from these real causes as the human eye can reach. Long before a husband has committed adultery, for instance, the divorce germ has entered his consciousness; long before a wife actually runs away from her husband, the seed of divorce has begun to take root in her mind. A hundred little things preface a husband's beating his wife, and so giving her grounds for divorce in certain States, as a hundred little things, which the investigators dismiss as negligible, preface a wife's running off to Paris with the first available chauffeur. What are these little things? Let me guess at a few.

Perhaps one of the chief causes of divorce, or, more exactly, leading up to the act or acts legally recognized as grounds for divorce, is a trivial physical blemish in one or the other of the parties to the marriage. This defect, in the husband's or the wife's person, may be comparatively insignificant, yet no matter. Such a blemish, when lived with for a period of time, has a cruel and devastating habit of burning itself into the eye and consciousness of the other person; it gradually becomes almost a visual phobia; its image will not out. It colors the one person's entire picture of the other; it grows to dominate that picture completely. In time, if the other person is at all sensitive—and four out of five persons are extremely sensitive in this respect—it becomes unbearable. The husband, if it be the husband, begins, almost unconsciously, to look around him at other and theoretically more immaculate women. The look grows steadier . . . Miami . . . the divorce court. Or he deserts his wife, or treats her with cruelty. The wife, on the other hand, if it be the wife, simply gets to the point where she cannot endure the marriage relation any longer, and leaves her husband's bed and board. And the newspapers, in due course, print the ground for divorce, but fail to print the reason. Another reason for the act or acts leading to divorce may be found in the inability of the married parties to stand the æsthetic jars that propinquity forces more or less upon them. This is particularly true of men and women who marry after the twenties have passed into the thirties. Such men and such women have grown so accustomed to physical and emotional independence that the habit is not easy to break. It is much more difficult for them to endure the invasions upon privacy that marriage brings with it than it is for younger persons. For every couple that have been put asunder by adultery, or lack of support, or a carpet-beater, there are two that have split by being compelled to use the same bathroom, or by a bathroom that was too disquietingly close to their bed-chamber. There are dozens of other such reasons, each and all overpowering in their superficial triviality. The two that have been set down are perhaps sufficient to suggest many of the rest. A marriage that has weathered stormy seas all too often goes to smash on a pebble.

§ 14

It takes, as they say, all kinds of men to make a world. Toward most of these, although there are many I may not accurately know or understand, I am sympathetic. I at least try to know them and understand them. But there is one kind that passes my comprehension altogether. This kind, try as I will, I cannot filter through my noodle. It is made up of the men who, though they are in love with no one woman and though they are comfortably off in health and in the world's goods, yet view marriage as something they should presently and duly embrace.

§ 15

Love demands infinitely less than friendship.

§ 16

That marriage mellows and civilizes the average man, I do not gainsay. But that is precisely my objection to it so far as I personally am concerned. I am already too highly civilized. Were it not for the overdose of civilization that has been inculcated in me, and that works so often to my economic and spiritual disadvantage, I should doubtless have been married long ago. To ask a man already civilized to get civilized all over again is like asking him to wear two undershirts. I dispute, further, that marriage would benefit my spirit, as certain of my friends and other enemies argue. It would make me too happy, and I could not do my work if I were too happy. A persistent touch of melancholy is essential to artistic enterprise. A happy man may be a successful bishop, dog-catcher, movie actor or sausage-monger, but no happy man ever produced a single first-rate piece of painting, sculpture, music or literature. And I, humble as I am, have aspirations.

Again, it is inconceivable that any woman, once she penetrated my superficial charms, could be devoted to me in the rôle of husband. Never was there such an ignoble crank! If, after ten mellifluous years of marriage and after giving birth to our fourteenth beautiful child, my loving wife were one day to so much as snitch a favorite lead-pencil off my writing-table, I should probably proceed forthwith to the big scene from "The Chinatown Trunk Mystery". I am not designed for marriage any more than a longshoreman is designed for Christian Science. I have no gift for it. I admire women and I like children, but is it necessary for a man who admires baseball, for example, to play baseball? It is not. I elect to view marriage from a seat in the bleachers.

Still again, we have the theory that marriage is insurance against the evils of romance; that it makes a man safe, and secure, and comfortable. The average bachelor, it is contended by way of proof, is never in as good health as the average benedick. This may be true; but it proves nothing. So far as that goes, I have never known a bachelor who was in as good health as the average mule.

§ 17

Love, Dr. Mencken once argued in the course of a conversation which happened to be engaging us at Muldoon's Health Farm at 5 A. M., is a casual matter, a chance infection, a thing not unlike a cold in the head. "The process of falling in love", he observed, "is as fortuitous and trivial as the process of missing a train. Some fair one, hearing that one has recently received an LL.D. from Yale or made a killing at some swindle, goes to a beauty parlor, has her eyebrows gummed, puts on her best frock, and then leers at one across a dinner-table. The result, by a well-known psychological route, is the genesis of the idea that she has lovely eyes and a beautiful character, and that it would be charming to give her a hug. Or maybe the thing is pure accident. Perhaps she goes to the party without the slightest thought of serious professional business—and one is floored by the perfume she happens to wear, or by her anecdote of her little nephew, Lafcadio, or by the pretty way she takes it when the Colonel upsets his *potage Arlesienne* down her leg, or by the peculiar manner in which her hair is banged, or by the striking combination of cerise and pea-green in her fourth-best party dress. Such is love, a madness worse than hydrophobia. To say that a man should be in love when he marries is to say that a ship-captain should be doubled up with cramps when he steers down the Ambrose Channel. It is a folly".

Although I am not the authority on love that my friend, the affable professor, is—as I politely confided to him at the time while four low Irish-

men were running a cold squirt-hose up and down
our backs—I permit myself to disagree with him.
If falling in love is as easy as he says it is—and
has personally demonstrated it to be on at least
eleven occasions during the last fiscal year—I have
the honor to set myself down as a duffer.   No less
than one thousand times in my life have I assidu-
ously tried to fall in love, but to be baffled.   All
the time that I have been eloquently trying to convince myself that the girl eating dinner at my expense was a divine mélange of Debussy, apri-
cots and chiffon, some irrepressible bogle within
me has confounded me with the hypothesis that
she was merely another Patou gown that hadn't
had enough lunch.   My imagination and my
intelligence meet, to my sorrow, at an eternal
Château-Thierry.   I have thus far fallen in love,
during the forty-odd years of my life, with twenty-
seven lace and linen baby collars, eighteen bobbed
hairs, forty-three blue dresses, ten lisps, thirty-six
pairs of hands on my forehead when I was down
with neuralgia, and eleven dozen initialed handkerchiefs and laundry bags, but with not a single
girl.   What, therefore, am I to do about it?   I
am helpless.   And to ask me to marry a girl
I don't love is to ask me to go to Buffalo when I
have business in Chattanooga.

§ 18

No marriage can be a successful and happy one which calls upon the man to change his ideas of what constitutes amusement after his day's work is done. If a man whose idea of pleasure after working hours is strip poker or playing a snare drum loves a woman passionately and marries her only to learn that her idea of pleasure in the same hours is Old Maid or Kelly pool, a time-table to Reno, if the man is a gentleman, or one to Atlantic City, if he is not, will be found on the drawing-room table before the year is over.

§ 19

To ask a man to marry on the ground that it will safeguard and comfort him in his later years is to ask him to cut his throat on the ground that he may be down with Bright's disease in 1950.

§ 20

The happiest marriage is not that which defers disillusion, but that which admits it at the outset. Few marriages between completely adult men and women turn out unhappily. Age is happy; youth, unhappy. Illusion is the happiness of the heart; disillusion is the merriment of the mind.

§ 21

I long ago wrote a note to the effect that the man a young woman marries is almost always her second choice. I now beg leave to revise that note. The man a young woman marries is almost always her third choice, if that. Is there, by way of proof, a single young woman in America who would not kick out the man she is to marry, whatever his position in her affections, if the Prince of Wales wanted her for his wife?

§ 22

It is the belief of most persons that a bachelor has a much happier time of it in this world than his married brother. Nothing could be farther from the truth. The married man's misery is confined to one woman. The bachelor's emotional aches spread over a dozen or more.

§ 23

Back of all the romantic blather about Uhuhu, Ahahaha, Umhumha and the other South Sea island maidens in whose amiable embraces the Anglo-Saxon heroes of current fictional *opera* find at length the peace and solace and comfort that have been denied them in paler embraces nearer home, there is, I have a notion, a soupçon of disconcerting truth. A man, as I have observed before, is always happiest with a woman who is deferentially his inferior. It is the equality of woman to man in the Anglo-Saxon countries—and not only the equality, but often actually the superiority—that is the cause of man's frequent dissatisfaction with his married lot and of the consequent alarming increase in the divorce rate. A marriage in which the wife knows the difference between a sonata and a *Geburtslied*, the distinction between second growth Pichon-Longueville and fifth growth Mouton d'Armailhacq, the relative eminence of George Eliot and George Barr McCutcheon, and the batting average of Babe Ruth, is already on its way to consult a shyster lawyer. The most successful marriage is ever the one in which the wife believes the husband to be a compendium of all the refinements of wisdom and understanding, however depressing an ass the husband may really be. And as in marriage, so in love. Since the discovery of ink, there is no record of an Anglo-Saxon's having divorced, for example, a Japanese wife.

§ 24

What a man beyond the years of forty seeks in the woman he marries is less an instrument of future happiness than a bulwark and haven against future unhappiness and disappointments. He chooses his wife not for the better in the years to come, but for the worse. He sees in her not so much a companion for his days of joy as a sympathetic companion for his days of sorrow. He sees her not in terms of music, moonlight and roses but in terms of mother-woman, heart-nurse and guarantee against the loneliness of unromantic old age.

§ 25

I have a theory that no intelligent man ever loves a woman truly until he knows her so well that he doesn't really see her when he talks to her—that is, until she ceases to arrest his actual attention. What he talks to thereafter is an artificiality created by his own imagination. If the woman is clever, she quickly converts herself into this artificiality, or, at all events, tries to do so. If she succeeds, the man is lost. His ideal has him by the ear.

§ 26

Love is an emotion experienced by the many and enjoyed by the few.

§ 27

The bravery of women!   How hard they strive to love the men they marry!

THE END

A NOTE ON THE TYPE IN
WHICH THIS BOOK IS SET

This book is composed on the Linotype in Bodoni, so-called after its designer, Giambattista Bodoni (1740–1813) a celebrated Italian scholar and printer. Bodoni planned his type especially for use on the more smoothly finished papers that came into vogue late in the eighteenth century and drew his letters with a mechanical regularity that is readily apparent on comparison with the less formal old style. Other characteristics that will be noted are the square serifs without fillet and the marked contrast beween the light and heavy strokes.

SET UP, ELECTROTYPED AND PRINTED BY THE VAIL-BALLOU PRESS, INC., BING-HAMTON, N. Y. · ESPARTO PAPER MANUFACTURED IN SCOTLAND AND FURNISHED BY W. F. ETHER-INGTON & CO., NEW YORK. BOUND BY H. WOLFF ESTATE, NEW YORK.